SAT 2-Second Shortcuts

the fastest route to SAT answers

Dr. Jay's Top 10 Shortcuts

SCORE FAST
0:02 0:00

PICK UP 100 EXTRA POINTS

INSTANTLY IMPROVE YOUR SCORE

THE BEST KEPT SECRETS IN SAT PREP ARE HERE

SEE WHAT YOU HAVE BEEN MISSING ▶▶▶▶▶▶

Carol Jay Stratoudakis, PhD

Frederick Fell Publishers, Inc
2131 Hollywood Blvd., Suite 305
Hollywood, Fl 33020

Printed in the United States of America.

14 13 12 11 10 9 8 7 6 5 4 3 2 1

Library of Congress Cataloging-in-Publication Data

Stratoudakis, Carol Jay.
  The SAT shortcut handbook : SAT 2-second shortcuts : the fastest route to SAT answers : Dr. Jay's top 10 shortcuts / Carol Jay Stratoudakis, Ph.D.
     pages cm
  ISBN 978-0-88391-281-2
  1. SAT (Educational test)--Study guides. I. Title.
  LB2353.57.S767 2014
  378.1'662--dc23
                        2014029038

For information about special discounts for bulk purchases, please contact Frederick Fell Special Sales at business@fellpublishers.com or call 945-455-4243.

ISBN-13   978-0-88391-281-2
eBook ISBN   9780883912829

To my parents

Acknowledgements

First and foremost, I would like to thank my husband Jim and my son Alex whose constant love and support made this book possible.

I am enormously thankful to my agent, Gina Panettieri, who guided this project through many incarnations with sage advice and endless energy.

To Brette McWhorter Sember, brilliant editor and stellar person, thank you for always knowing what is missing, what is superfluous, and how to fix everything.

Thank you to the dynamic team at Frederick Fell Publishers, Inc. To Don Lessne, for your direction at every milestone; and to Kelly Apgar, for your perspective and watchful eye. To Ravi Gupta and the super-talented team at TechnicaCon, thank you for your top-notch interior design; and to Jacinta Calcut at Image Graphics Design, thank you for creating the perfect cover for this book.

Special thanks to family and friends for so much encouragement: Gary Colello and Patti Colello, Joyce Rechtschaffen and Lloyd Guerci, Kristen Lohser, Paige Panda, Julia Bartlett, Cynthia Turner, Rose Hayden, Al Domroe, Len Perlman, John Rotante, Jerry Rotante, Marian Fink, Sumbal Liaquat, Bobbie Olson, Kimberly MacDonald, and Elaine Stephens.

Finally, thank you to all my students who inspired me to find a way to simplify the SAT.

Attention:
Parents, Tutors, and Coaches

Your students will *stress less* and *score more* points when they go to their SAT test with all their test-taking skills **PLUS** a set of SAT Shortcuts that gives them a fast-scoring strategy to collect the **50-100 additional points** they need to reach their SAT GOAL:

- ◗ *A high enough score* to be admitted to the college your students would most like to attend.
- ◗ *A high enough score* to qualify for a scholarship.
- ◗ *A high enough score* to be recruited to play a college sport.

Your students will thank you for a book that:

- ◗ Puts a simple, analytical strategy in their hands that works faster than the process of elimination (POE),
- ◗ Gives them instant opportunities to increase their score they never saw before, and
- ◗ Requires NO STUDYING to learn. Only 15 minutes of rapid scanning practice is needed to know how to use a Shortcut.

Think of me as "The Dr. Mom of SAT Shortcuts." Together, we can ensure your student goes to the SAT armed with a set of Shortcuts to answer more SAT questions, collect more points, and *close the 50 - 100 point gap* between a current PSAT or SAT score and the higher score your student is aiming to achieve.

Check in with me at **info@DrJaySATShortcuts.com**. I am as ready as you are to give your students *the easiest strategy to answer SAT questions.*

Dr. Jay

Table of Contents

Shortcuts #1, #2, and #3: Practice locating these 3 Shortcuts to instantly predict the answers.

Introduction

Success in life is about acting on opportunity. Success on the SAT is about acting on all the *opportunities* the Shortcuts give you to increase your score 100 points or more – enough to **close the gap** between the SAT score you currently have and the SAT score you want for college admission.

The 10 Shortcuts in this book put an end to the "old school" thinking that there are no quick and easy Shortcuts to success on the SAT. This thinking is **completely false!** Each Shortcut opens your eyes to opportunities you have never seen before to quickly and easily **increase your score — *without studying***. Only rapid scanning practice is required to learn how to instantly recognize Shortcuts to answer SAT questions as fast as you click on Google or tap an app on a smartphone.

It is time to **STOP** passively following the "old school" advice to skip all the SAT questions that look too hard to answer and **START** proactively following Dr. Jay's Golden Rule to answer more hard questions, collect more points, and increase your SAT score.

DR. JAY'S GOLDEN RULE

Before you start to use the process of elimination (POE) to answer a question or decide to skip a question, **ALWAYS take 2 seconds to look for a Shortcut to the answer.**

SAT: 2 Second Shortcuts are the best-kept secrets to success on the SAT test that you will not find in any other test prep book or course. You owe it to yourself today to **SEE THE REAL SHORTCUTS TO SUCCESS on the SAT test you have been missing in all your practice tests and previous SAT tests.**

PART I
THE POWER OF THE SHORTCUTS

Shortcuts

SHORTCUTS

Whoever You Are, the Shortcuts Work for You

No matter who you are, when you are taking the SAT, or what SAT score you are aiming to achieve, the Shortcuts are for you. The Shortcuts give *every* student taking the SAT the fastest and easiest route to more correct SAT answers and a higher score.

You are a senior taking the SAT for the second time

You took the SAT last spring, now you are taking it again this fall. On your last practice SAT test, your score remained the same, give or take a few points. You know if you keep preparing for the SAT in exactly the same way as you did before, you are likely to get the same results. You need to add another strategy to your skill set to bump your score to a higher level. You would like to increase your score 50 points or more to reach the average SAT score for admission to the colleges and universities you would most like to attend. The Shortcuts give you exactly what you need: *a second chance* to score more points by spotting Shortcuts to the answers that you never knew existed in SAT questions.

You are a junior taking the SAT for the first time

You are taking the SAT for the first time this spring. You went online and registered, then took a big gulp after committing to the test date. Now you are seriously starting to prep for the test. You know a few Shortcuts to answer math questions, but you have never learned any Shortcuts to help you answer reading and writing questions. In reading sections that include long passages, you would definitely like to have a set of Shortcuts at your fingertips to answer the 24 questions you are given 25 minutes to answer. Of course, you want to pace yourself and you do not want to rush, but you know that the more questions you can answer correctly under the time limit, the more points you collect, and the higher your score.

You are an athlete competing for a spot on a college team

Your coach has told you that you need to break 500 or better in reading and math on the SAT to be considered for admission or to be eligible for an athletic scholarship. You know the value of speed in your sport, and you want the competitive advantages the Shortcuts give you when you are up against the pressure of the SAT time clock and competing with other athletes to reach the SAT cut off score you need.

You are a high school scholar aspiring to attend an Ivy League school

You are challenging yourself to excel in AP or IB courses, earn the highest possible GPA, and get a high enough SAT score to be considered for admission to the top colleges and universities in the U.S., including the Ivy League. You know you need to increase your SAT reading score by 50 points to reach the average score earned by the students who were recently accepted to the Ivy League school you would most like to attend. Every time you take another practice test, you keep getting the same reading score. You realize if you keep doing the same thing you have always done to answer questions you are likely to keep getting the same results. You wish you had an extra scoring strategy that would make it easier for you to collect the extra 50 points you need.

You are a foreign student aspiring to earn an undergraduate degree from a college or university in the United States

You are from another country. Your first language is not English. You want to have the Shortcuts at your fingertips because they reduce the amount of English you have to read in a question. Instead of reading and thinking about 5 answer choices, you only have to read and think about 2 or 3 answer choices. When you use the Shortcuts in this book to answer questions on your SAT, you gain a huge competitive advantage over other students around the world. They will have to read and think about more information in English, while you will read and think about less.

You are a procrastinator

We all put off doing difficult things, like studying for the SAT, in favor of doing fun things. If you like playing video games, you can put the scanning skills you have developed playing *Call of Duty* or *Angry Birds* to use on your SAT. If you normally cram for tests and actually do well when you study at the last minute for a big exam, the Shortcuts are made for you. Select 3 Shortcuts you think would be most helpful to you and learn them in 1 hour, then use them on a practice test to see how fast the Shortcuts work to help you get the minimum score you need to be considered for admission to a college or university on your list.

The Shortcut BREAKTHROUGH Strategy

All you have to do to increase your SAT score is *BREAK OUT* of *only* using the process of elimination (POE) to answer SAT questions and *BREAK INTO also* using Shortcuts. As soon as you change how you start to answer SAT questions, you will experience the extra scoring power the Shortcuts give you to find answer faster than ever before possible. Time to:

 Stop thinking there are no quick and easy Shortcuts to success on the SAT.

 Start thinking there are 10 quick and easy Shortcuts to maximize your success on the SAT.

 Stop relying *only* on the longer process of elimination (POE) to answer *all* SAT questions.

 Start taking advantage of Shortcuts that give you a shorter process to answer more reading, writing and math SAT questions.

 Stop thinking all the information loaded into all 5 answer choices to a question is equally important.

 Start thinking that inside information in 2 (possibly 3) answer choices is often more important.

 Stop thinking that to answer an SAT question you *always* have to go through the process of thinking about all 5 possible answers to a question.

 Start thinking that to answer an SAT question you can sometimes focus your thinking on only 2 (possibly 3) answer choices that follow a distinct pattern.

Stop thinking that decisions made slowly and deliberately based on all the information available in all 5 answer choices are better than decisions made very quickly based on less information in 2 (possibly 3) answer choices.

 Start thinking that decisions made very quickly based on less information in 2 (possibly 3) answer choices are just as good as decisions made slowly and deliberately based on all the information available in all 5 answer choices.

 Stop thinking that in all life situations haste always makes waste.

 Start thinking on the SAT haste does not make waste. In 2 seconds, you can cut to the chase and decide on the 2 best answer choices to a test question.

 Stop seeing 5 *random* answer choices to SAT questions.

 Start seeing distinct patterns in the 5 answer choices.

The Shortcut strategy forever changes how you START to answer SAT questions by **concentrating your thinking for the first time on analyzing distinct patterns in the answer choices.** Now the shortest distance between an **SAT QUESTION** and an **SAT ANSWER** is a Shortcut in this book that follows a simple, easily detectable pattern hidden in the answer choices.

POE: The Longer Strategy

SAT Question _____*SAT Answer*

- ▶▶ The question is longer and harder to answer and the process is slower.
- ▶▶ The process relies on more time-consuming, deliberate thinking.
- ▶▶ The process requires reading and thinking about all 5 answer choices to answer a question.

SHORTCUTS: The Shorter Strategy

SAT Question _____*SAT Answer*

- ▶▶ The question is shorter and easier to answer and the process is faster.
- ▶▶ The process relies on less time-consuming, on-the-spot thinking.
- ▶▶ The process requires reading and thinking about only 2 (possibly 3) answer choices to answer a question.

Two questions I always ask my students are:

- ▶▶ When you are under the time pressure of the SAT, why would you take the time to use the slower POE route to get to the answer, if there is a faster, more direct route to the answer?
- ▶▶ Why not save yourself time, energy, and effort on the SAT by using Shortcuts to answer as many questions as possible, and then rely on POE to answer all the questions that do not contain a Shortcut?

My students tell me the questions are no-brainers! First, they always look for a Shortcut to find answers fast. When no Shortcut is in sight, then they use the slower process of elimination (POE). **SHORTCUTS + POE = the WINNING COMBINATION of strategies to maximize success on the SAT.**

The Shortcut TOP SECRET PATTERNS

The power of the Shortcuts is in the **secret patterns.** The Shortcuts speed up the process of elimination (POE) by instantly pointing out to you patterns hidden inside the answer choices to SAT questions. The instant you detect a pattern, this inside information makes it possible for you to cut to the chase and make a prediction: **When 2 (possibly 3) answer choices follow a simple, easy to detect pattern, then 1 of the answer choices is most likely the correct answer to a SAT question.** As a result, in 2 seconds you can go directly to the 2 (possibly 3) best answer choices to an SAT question, focus your thinking on deciding between these choices, and instantly have in plain sight the best chance you can get to score on the SAT.

Many patterns in the answer choices isolate the 2 best answer choices that give you a 50% chance to score a point, some patterns isolate 3 answer choices that give you a 33% chance to score a point, and sometimes a pattern identifies the 1 best answer choice that gives you a near 100% chance to score a point.

Teachers, tutors, and test prep courses have never taught you how to analyze the answer choices to SAT questions to detect **secret patterns** that shortcut the process of answering SAT questions. They have always believed that there are no quick and easy Shortcuts to answering SAT questions and that increasing your SAT score is a gradual, incremental process. While in many situations in life, the best strategy usually is slow and steady wins the race, the **secret patterns** in SAT questions change this reality. Now there is a strategy to winning the race and reaching your goal on the SAT that values speed and places a premium on instant decision-making.

All the Shortcuts in this book are based on the belief that decisions make very quickly by recognizing a pattern in the answer choices are just as good as decisions made more slowly and deliberately by reading and thinking about all the information in the answer choices. Athletes, coaches, doctors, military leaders, musicians, and many others make snap decisions based on patterns they instantly recognize from their experience and instincts; now you as a test-taker can make snap decisions on the SAT based on the patterns you instantly recognize from your experience learning all the Shortcuts in this book.

The Shortcut INSTANT SCORING ADVANTAGES

The instant you detect a simple pattern in the answer choices to an SAT question, you get the fastest route to an SAT answer, PLUS you collect 5 INSTANT SCORING ADVANTAGES no other SAT strategy offers you:

 INSTANT SCORING ADVANTAGE #1: Reduce Answer Choices from 5 to 2

Most Shortcuts cut the answer choices to an SAT question down from 5 possibilities to the 2 best answer choices, wiping out confusing and irrelevant information loaded into the answer choices to distract your attention from the best answer choices. *No other strategy* makes it possible for you to answer a SAT question <u>without thinking</u> about ALL the possible answers and instantly hands you the 2 best answer choices.

 INSTANT SCORING ADVANTAGE #2: Reduce the Difficulty of SAT Questions

Since the Shortcuts put the 2 best answer choices in sharp focus for you, they immediately **reduce the difficulty of SAT questions**. A question with only 2 answer choices to read and think about before making a decision is far less difficult than a question with 5 answer choices to read and think about before making a decision.

 INSTANT SCORING ADVANTAGE #3: Save Time, Effort, and Mental Energy

Every time you use a Shortcut to answer a question, you save all the time it would normally take you to complete the process of elimination (POE) — anywhere from 20 to 30 seconds per question. This is a huge savings when you are under the pressure of the SAT clock. **The more time you save by using Shortcuts, the more time you gain to answer all the questions in your test that do not have a Shortcut to the answer.**

 INSTANT SCORING ADVANTAGE #4: Turn Tough Questions You Previously Omitted into Scoring Opportunities

Now you can go to your SAT with a strategy that gives you the **ability to answer many questions** you previously omitted on your test, including:

- ▸▸ Questions you had no clue how to begin to answer
- ▸▸ Questions you skipped because they looked intimidating
- ▸▸ Questions you never had time to go back to answer

Instead of passively leaving all these questions blank, you proactively look for a Shortcut to the answer.

 INSTANT SCORING ADVANTAGE #5: Stress Less Today and on Test Day

The Shortcuts dramatically **reduce your stress today** because they give you a simple strategy to attack all the hard questions you dread seeing on your SAT and previously thought you had to skip. Instead of worrying about all the hard questions you will face, you are psyched to use Dr. Jay's Golden Rule to cut through all your stress and empower you to turn hard questions into much easier questions to answer. **THE GOLDEN RULE: Always take 2 seconds to look for a Shortcut to the answer that will give you an instant chance to score.**

On test day, you walk into your test more in control of a stressful situation because you have 2 strategies to answer questions: SHORTCUTS *plus* POE. Your plan is to **FIRST look for a Shortcut** that will give you the fastest route to the answer BEFORE you start to use POE. If you do not spot a Shortcut in 2 seconds, then you know you can count on the traditional, longer process of elimination (POE) to answer a question.

The Shortcut FAST 50 POINT PLAN

It is important to set a realistic goal. How much you can increase your SAT score depends upon your starting point and how much effort you put into learning the Shortcuts. For starters, aim to reach a score that is **50 points higher than the score you received on your PSAT or a recent SAT.** Fifty points is often *the all-important gap closer* between the score you currently have on your PSAT or a recent SAT and the score you need to reach.

Adding 50 points to your score is enough to make or break your chances for college admission, for a scholarship, and for eligibility to play a college sport. For example, if you are at 450 or slightly above and the college coach says you have to break 500 to meet the eligibility requirement for admission, then 50 points will make a big difference in your college future.

Check the Sample Reading Score Conversion Table on the next page to find the number of raw points that corresponds with a reading SAT goal of 500. Notice you have to collect a total of 30 (raw) points in reading which means you have to correctly answer 30 questions. The 30 (raw) points roughly converts to a SAT (scaled) score of 500.

Sample SAT Reading Score Conversion Table

Raw Score	Scaled Score
65	800
63	750
57	700
53	650
46	600
38	550
30	500
22	450
14	400

How 50 Points Add Up FAST

USE   **10 Shortcuts to answer 10 questions**

GET   **5 correct answers**

By the law of chance (like flipping a coin) you are likely to get 5 out of 10 questions correct (50%).

COLLECT   **5 raw points:**

5 (raw points) × 10 (points per question) = 50 Points.

After you collect your first 50 points, you can then move on to find your next 10 Shortcuts to add another 50 points to your score.

Setting Your Goal

While the math SAT score is important to students who wish to obtain degrees in math or science, the reading SAT score is important to all students. All colleges and universities want their students to be able to read and write at a college level. Because of this, the examples below for increasing your score are all related to increasing your reading score 50 points at a time.

 Starting SAT Goal: Raise Your Reading Score from 450 to 500

If your starting goal is to reach 500, then as the Conversion Table on page 10 indicates, you need to get 30 correct answers in reading to score 30 (raw) points that will convert to a total (scaled) score of 500. To reach the goal of 500, plan to answer at least 36 questions out of the total 67 reading questions on the test. This allows you to miss questions and still reach your goal. Use as many Shortcuts as you can find to collect all the points you need.

After you attempt to answer 36 questions, take any remaining time to scan the questions you did not answer for Shortcuts to add 1 or 2 more points to your score.

 Starting Goal: Raise Your Reading Scaled Score from 500 to 550

If your starting goal is to reach 550, then as the Conversion Table on page 10 indicates, you need to get 38 correct answers to score 38 (raw) points that will convert to a total (scaled) score of 550. To reach your goal of 550, plan to answer at least 44 questions out of the total 67 reading questions on the test. This allows you to miss questions and still reach your goal. Use as many Shortcuts as you can find to collect all the points you need.

After you attempt to answer 44 questions, take any remaining time to scan the questions you did not answer for Shortcuts to add 1 or 2 more points to your score.

 Starting Goal: Raise Your Scaled Score from 550 to 600

If your starting goal is to reach 600, then as the Conversion Table on page 10 indicates, you need to get 46 correct answers to score 46 (raw) points that will convert to a total (scaled) score of 600. To reach your goal of 600, plan to answer at least 52 questions of the total 67 reading questions in the test. This allows you to miss questions and still reach your goal. Use as many Shortcuts as you can find to collect all the points you need.

After you attempt to answer 52 questions, use any remaining time to scan the questions you did not answer for Shortcuts to add 1 or 2 more points to your score.

Starting Goal: Raise Your Scaled Score from 600 to 650

If your starting goal is to reach 650, then as the Conversion Table on page 10 indicates, you need to get 53 correct answers on the test to score 53 (raw) points that will convert to a total (scaled) score of 650. To reach your goal of 650, plan to answer at least 59 questions of the total 67 reading questions on the test. This allows you to miss questions and still reach your goal. Use as many Shortcuts as you can find to collect all the points you need.

After you attempt to answer 59 questions, take any remaining time to scan the questions you have not answered for Shortcuts to add 1 or 2 more points to your score.

Starting Goal: Raise Your Reading Scaled Score from 650 to 700

If your starting goal is to reach 700, then as the Conversion Table on page 10 indicates, you need to get 57 correct answers to score 57 (raw) points that will convert to a total (scaled) score of 700. To reach your goal of 700, plan to answer at least 63 questions of the total 67 reading questions on the test. This allows you to miss questions and still reach your goal. Use as many Shortcuts as you can find to collect all the points you need.

After you attempt to answer at least 63 questions, take any remaining time to scan the questions you did not answer for Shortcuts to add 1 or 2 more points to your score.

Starting SAT Goal: Raise Your Reading Score from 700 to 750+

If your goal is to score 750 or higher, than as the Conversion Table on page 10 indicates, you need to get 63 or more correct answers in reading to score 63 (raw) points that will convert to a total (scaled) score of 750. To reach the goal of 750, plan to answer all 67 reading questions on the test. This allows you to miss just a few questions and still reach your goal. Use as many Shortcuts as you can find to collect all the points you need.

After you attempt to answer all 67 questions, check your answers to be sure you used all the Shortcuts for an instant chance to score.

How the Shortcut Strategy Works

After you read a SAT question, the **first thing** you do is take 2 seconds to scan the 5 answer choices to spot a **secret pattern** that gives you a **Shortcut** to the answer.

This new first step draws upon your rapid scanning skills to detect a Shortcut in the answer choices. To develop your ability to find Shortcuts in 2 seconds, it is important to:

❯❯ Know WHAT Shortcuts you can expect to see in the reading, writing, and math sections of your SAT.

❯❯ Know WHERE the Shorcuts will be located in the answer choices to SAT questions.

❯❯ Practice scanning SAT questions to snap up Shortcuts in just seconds.

❯❯ Use the Shortcuts to answer questions in every SAT practice test you take.

Think of me as your SAT Shortcut Coach. I am now going to take you inside the SAT to see 10 different secret patterns hidden in plain sight that will give you all the Shortcuts you need to quickly collect an EXTRA 50 to 100 points and achieve EXTRAordinary results on your SAT – without studying. As you will see, only 15 minutes of scanning practice is required to initially master a Shortcut in this book.

PART II
TOP SECRET SHORTCUTS

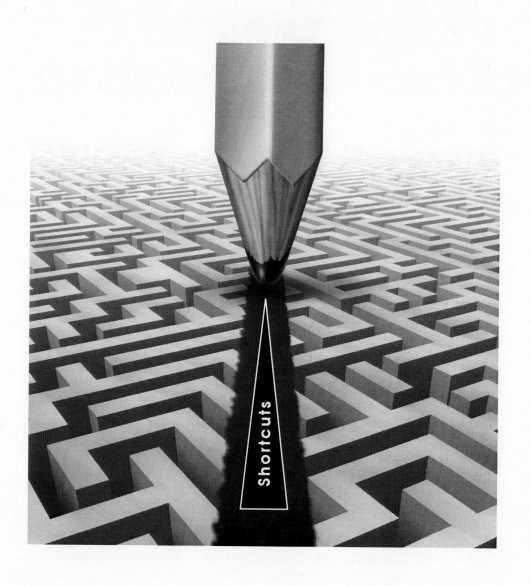

Shortcuts

READING SHORTCUT #1

SECRET PATTERN:

2 ANSWER CHOICES that START with the SAME WORD(S):

(A) xxxxxxxxxxxxxxxxxxxxxxxxxx

(B) carriage xxxxxxxxxxxxxxxxx

(C) xxxxxxxxxxxxxxxxxxxxxxxxx

(D) carriage xxxxxxxxxxxxxxxxx

(E) xxxxxxxxxxxxxxxxxxxxxxxxx

Before you start to use the process of elimination (POE) to answer an SAT reading question or decide to skip a question, take **2 seconds** to look for this **secret pattern**: *2 answer choices that start with the same word(s).*

DETECT

2 answer choices (we'll call them X and Y) that start with the same word(s).

PREDICT

X or Y is the correct answer.

Rule out the other answer choices!

DECIDE

either X or Y.

If you are clueless, just pick X or Y. You have a **50% chance** to select the correct answer – without thinking about either choice!

If you have a clue to tip your decision in favor of X or Y, you have a **much higher than 50% chance** to select the correct answer.

SCORE

| 1 correct answer | *gives you* | 1(raw) point |
| 1 (raw) point | *roughly adds* | 10 points to your SAT score! |

The following 3 examples of Shortcut #1 are SNAPSHOTS that show you how extremely easy it is to recognize the secret pattern Shortcut #1 is based on: **2 answer choices that start with the same word(s).**

Example #1: BEFORE

Before you recognize the Shortcut, the SAT question is **difficult**. It is longer and harder to answer with 5 possible answers to read and think about.

1. The reference to breakfast cereal bars (lines 16-21) supports the position that

   (A) claims of nutritional value are questionable
   (B) cereal bars are no substitute for a hot breakfast
   (C) limited research is used to make broad statements
   (D) claims of health benefits inflate product price
   (E) the contents of "healthy snacks" need to be evaluated

Example #1: AFTER

After you recognize the Shortcut, the question is **simple**. It is shorter and easier to answer with only 2 possible answers to read and think about.

1. The reference to breakfast cereal bars (lines 16-21) supports the position that

   (A) claims of nutritional value are questionable
   (D) claims of health benefits inflate product price

In 2 seconds, Shortcut #1 turns a hard question you skipped on your last SAT into an easy question you can answer on your next SAT.

Before you start to use the process of elimination (POE) to answer an SAT question or decide to skip a question, take *2 seconds* to scan the answer choices for this **secret pattern:** *2 answer choices that start with the same word(s).*

DETECT

"claims of" in **(A) and (D).**

PREDICT

(A) or (D) is the correct answer.

Rule out the other answer choices!

DECIDE

either (A) or (D).

When you are totally clueless, just pick (A) or (D).

By the law of chance, you get a **great 50% chance** to select the correct answer.

When you have a clue to tip your decision in favor of (A) or (D), go for it.

By using a bit of knowledge, you get a **much higher than 50% chance** to select the correct answer.

SCORE

| 1 correct answer | *gives you* | 1(raw) point |
| 1 (raw) point | *roughly adds* | 10 points to your SAT score! |

Example #2: BEFORE

Before you recognize the Shortcut, the SAT question is **difficult**. It is longer and harder to answer with 5 possible answers to read and think about.

2. In line 26, the quotation marks around the word "usual" serve to

    (A) emphasize the unusual style of the author's writing
    (B) suggest disapproval of a stereotype
    (C) emphasize the weakness of a neutral statement
    (D) call attention to the secondary meaning of a term
    (E) stress the importance of this word in context

Example #2: AFTER

After you recognize the Shortcut, the question is **simple**. It is shorter and easier to answer with only 2 possible answers to read and think about.

2. In line 26, the quotation marks around the word "usual" serve to

    (A) emphasize the unusual style of the author's writing
    (C) emphasize the weakness of a neutral statement

Before you start to use the process of elimination (POE) to answer an SAT question or decide to skip a question, take *2 seconds* to scan the answer choices for this **secret pattern**: *2 answer choices that start with the same word(s).*

DETECT

"emphasize the" in **(A)** and **(C)**.

PREDICT

(A) or (C) is the correct answer.

Rule out the other answer choices!

DECIDE

either (A) or (C).

When you are totally clueless, just pick (A) or (C).
By the law of chance, you get a **great 50% chance** to select the correct answer.

When you have a clue to tip your decision in favor of (A) or (C), go for it.
By using a bit of knowledge, you get a **much higher than 50% chance** to select the correct answer.

SCORE

1 correct answer	*gives you*	1 (raw) point
1 (raw) point	*roughly adds*	10 points to your SAT score!

Example #3: BEFORE

Before you recognize the Shortcut, the SAT question is **difficult**. It is longer and harder to answer with 5 possible answers to read and think about.

3. The author mentions the film *Midnight in Paris* (line 23) primarily to

   (A) capture a romantic view of the city
   (B) introduce different French literary figures
   (C) provide an example of a flashback
   (D) suggest that Paris is magical at night
   (E) introduce the reader to time travel

Example #3: AFTER

After you recognize the Shortcut, the question is **simple**. It is shorter and easier to answer with only 2 possible answers to read and think about.

3. The author mentions the film *Midnight in Paris* (line 23) primarily to

   (B) introduce different French literary figures
   (E) introduce the reader to time travel

Before you start to use the process of elimination (POE) to answer an SAT reading question or decide to skip a question, take *2 seconds* to scan the answer choices for this **secret pattern**: *2 answer choices that start with the same word(s).*

DETECT

"introduce" in (B) and (E).

PREDICT

(B) or (E) is the correct answer.

Rule out the other answer choices!

DECIDE

either (B) or (E).

When you are totally clueless, just pick (B) or (E).
By the law of chance, you get a **great 50% chance** to select the correct answer.

When you have a clue to tip your decision in favor of (B) or (E), go for it.
By using a bit of knowledge, you get a much **higher than 50% chance** to select the correct answer.

SCORE

| 1 correct answer | *gives you* | 1(raw) point |
| 1 (raw) point | *roughly adds* | 10 points to your SAT score! |

The POWER of KNOWING How to Analyze Answer Choices

After seeing Shortcut #1, you have the power of knowing exactly which **secret pattern** to look for in the answer choices that will give you an instant opportunity to score you never recognized before in SAT questions.

Shortcut #1: Speed Practice Drills

Now it is time to practice using Shortcut #1 to access opportunities to score on your SAT in *2 seconds – as fast as you click on Google or tap an app* on *your smartphone.* The questions in the following drills are designed to develop your ability to rapidly scan the answer choices to detect this Shortcut to the correct answers: *the same word(s) at the beginning of 2 answer choices.*

The repetition built into the 3 drills will make scanning the answer choices for Shortcut #1 a part of your test-taking routine – a new habit to SCORE FAST. The faster you can snap up Shortcut #1 in the following drills, the better prepared you will be to take advantage of this Shortcut on your SAT test.

Shortcut #1: Speed Practice Drill A

1. In lines 24-27, the narrator acknowledges which of the following points

   (A) test results require verification over time
   (B) observations should be substantiated by facts
   (C) scientific theories evolve through trial and error
   (D) research studies have unintended consequences
   (E) scientific discoveries disprove popular assumptions

2. The first paragraph of Passage 2 (lines 1-23) primarily addresses the potential conflict between

   (A) annual raises and fiscal responsibility
   (B) legal and illegal accounting procedures
   (C) family responsibility and financial goals
   (D) wealth and moral obligations
   (E) legal income and ethical behavior

3. The last 2 sentences of Passage 1 (lines 72-80) suggests that the narrator

   (A) recognizes that conflicts are rooted in ethnic beliefs
   (B) believes in the equal distribution of natural resources
   (C) thinks political unrest emerges from religious intolerance
   (D) believes that poverty increases hostilities between groups
   (E) assumes that economic inequality causes civil disputes

4. In the fourth paragraph (lines 45-58), the author makes the point that

   (A) last minute errors are costly to correct
   (B) editing is essential to ensure quality writing
   (C) ghostwriting is a unique skill valued by authors
   (D) editing affects the style of an essay
   (E) the table of contents is an outline of the text

5. The physician's assistant's critique (lined 32- 43) supports the position that

    (A) procedures can be more harmful than beneficial

    (B) medical practice should cure illness, not improve beauty

    (C) procedures advertised as "quick and easy" are misleading

    (D) insurance companies should not cover cosmetic surgery

    (E) face lifts have a positive psychological effect

6. The author references chemical companies (lines 49-55) in order to

    (A) call attention to manufacturers of harmful chemicals

    (B) illustrate that some companies protect the environment

    (C) provide examples of corporate compliance with regulations

    (D) raise concern about the disposal of industrial waste

    (E) provide examples of environmental protection

7. In lines 56-78, the travel agent makes the point that resorts and water parks

    (A) integrate water with family fun

    (B) are ideal summer vacation destinations

    (C) allow families to escape from the city

    (D) combine technology with recreational activities

    (E) integrate entertainment with relaxation

8. The description of American people as "well off" (line 32) is based on the belief that

    (A) the United States is the land of unlimited opportunity

    (B) Americans work hard and are paid well

    (C) the United States has a higher standard of living

    (D) immigrants can find good jobs in America

    (E) a capitalist society gives citizens access to wealth

9. The characterization of a typical "high school athlete" in line 59-64 underscores the narrator's concern about the

    (A) intense pressure placed on athletes to excel

    (B) decline of team spirit in high school

    (C) emphasis placed on winning at all cost

    (D) increase in the use of steroids

    (E) emphasis placed on speed in sports

10. The discussion of grocery shopping (lines 23-48) highlights the

    (A) father's attitude toward the family's new neighborhood

    (B) daughter's desire to assimilate into the American culture

    (C) tensions between two generations of immigrants

    (D) lack of ethnic food to prepare traditional meals

    (E) father's desire to preserve ancient customs

Check the Answer Key on the next page.

ANSWER KEY
Shortcut #1: Speed Practice Drill A

Best Choices		Answer
1.	C or E	E
2.	B or E	B
3.	B or D	B
4.	B or D	D
5.	A or C	A
6.	C or E	C
7.	A or E	A
8.	A or C	C
9.	C or E	C
10.	A or E	E

SCORE BOX

Correct Answers	Raw Points	Scaled Points
1	1	10
2	2	20
3	3	30
4	4	40
5	5	50
6	6	60
7	7	70
8	8	80
9	9	90
10	10	100

_____ Your Total   _____ Your Raw Points   _____ Points Added to Your SAT Score!

Shortcut #1: Speed Practice Drill B

Directions:

▶▶ Set your timer or timer app for 40 seconds.

▶▶ Underline the same word(s) at the beginning of 2 answer choices in each question.

▶▶ Circle 1 answer choice — without thinking about either choice.

Experience the awesome 50/50 chance you get to score a point the second you spot this Shortcut in the following questions.

1. The student council lost interest in the recycling project primarily because

   (A) students mixed soda cans with papers
   (B) not enough classrooms participated
   (C) custodians did not empty the bins
   (D) students found the project extremely time consuming
   (E) containers filled up faster than they could be emptied

2. It can be inferred from the passage that the flower arrangement

   (A) was not properly packed for delivery
   (B) could last a week indoors
   (C) needed to be trimmed in order to bloom
   (D) was left outdoors for too long
   (E) required fresh water and light

3. In paragraph 2 (lines 41-56), the man encouraged his nephew to live with him primarily because he

   (A) regretted not spending time with the boy
   (B) felt it was never too late to be a good uncle
   (C) thought he could be a role model
   (D) wanted to rescue his nephew from debt
   (E) thought he could offer emotional support

4. The author's assumption in the final paragraph (lines 62-67) is that

   (A) different people react in different ways
   (B) interpretations of paintings are driven by experience
   (C) responses to any art form are unpredictable
   (D) light triggers a range of emotional reactions
   (E) responses from men and women vary in intensity

5. Marian's perspective was different from "other women in New York" (lines 20-35) primarily because

   (A) life in the East was less demanding than life out West
   (B) her friend's difficulties made her constraints seem minor
   (C) she had more time to work in New York
   (D) her career was progressing outside the city
   (E) working was more important to her than socializing

6. In lines 51-58, the author's discussion of the Christmas tree suggests that

   (A) going into the woods evoked childhood memories
   (B) decorating the house was a cherished family tradition
   (C) the ritual provided an element of continuity with the past
   (D) the children appreciated the tree more in Canada than in Italy
   (E) the children thought Santa Claus brought all the presents

7. In Passage 1, "interactive" learning games (line 37-42) are mentioned to illustrate

   (A) how games appeal to different age groups
   (B) the variety of ways to sustain student attention
   (C) an engaging approach to classroom instruction
   (D) a powerful alternative to reading a textbook
   (E) how technology can be used to reach reluctant learners

8. The ad for the online dinner reservation service (lines 39-45) is cited in order to

   (A) persuade people to use the service
   (B) provide an alternative to "calling ahead"
   (C) provide an example of innovative social marketing
   (D) illustrate the value of a last minute convenience
   (E) compare different ways of making reservations

9. The author references technology in the third paragraph (lines 51-67) primarily to

   (A) suggest a vision for twenty-first century learning
   (B) observe the impact of cellphones in the classroom
   (C) argue that the internet will continue to change education
   (D) suggest an advancement in computer-based instruction
   (E) propose changes in teacher-student interaction

10. Both the author of Passage 1 and the author of Passage 2 acknowledge that

   (A) the Earth's supply of energy is limited
   (B) population estimates are unreliable
   (C) nonscientists do not test their assumptions
   (D) birth control is one option to limit growth
   (E) the Earth's resources are rapidly depleting

Check the Answer Key on the next page.

ANSWER KEY
Shortcut #1: Speed Practice Drill B

Best Choices	Answer
1. A or D	A
2. A or D	D
3. C or E	C
4. C or E	E
5. B or D	B
6. D or E	D
7. A or E	E
8. B or C	B
9. A or D	A
10. A or E	E

SCORE BOX

Correct Answers	Raw Points	Scaled Points
1	1	10
2	2	20
3	3	30
4	4	40
5	5	50
6	6	60
7	7	70
8	8	80
9	9	90
10	10	100

_____ Your Total   _____ Your Raw Points   _____ Points Added to Your SAT Score!

Shortcut #1: Speed Practice Drill C

1. Eric's decision not to share a room with Lloyd is primarily related to

   (A) his perception that they had nothing in common
   (B) their divergent class schedules
   (C) Lloyd's tendency to play loud music
   (D) differences in sleeping habits
   (E) his need for more personal space

2. The statement in lines 17-19 primarily indicates that the author of Passage 1 believes

   (A) women struggle with identity questions throughout life
   (B) men have fewer unresolved conflicts
   (C) gender issues peak during adolescence
   (D) men deal with conflicts through sports
   (E) college students are drawn to case studies

3. What does the author of Passage 1 believe is a major contributing factor to the decline in museum attendance?

   (A) the increase in admission charges
   (B) competition with multi-media displays
   (C) outdated exhibit formats
   (D) the disappearance of tour guides
   (E) competition with exhibits online

4. Madame Chloe's observations in lines 34-41 suggest that the owner of the jewelry store

   (A) was a trusted appraiser of estate jewelry
   (B) had a reputation for designing unique pendants
   (C) built long-term relationships with customers
   (D) had an appreciation for family heirlooms
   (E) attracted a broad range of clients

5. The last 2 sentences of Passage 1 (lines 72-81) suggest that the author

(A) favors community-based agencies that help veterans

(B) believes in expanding the role of mental health organizations

(C) values the outreach efforts of volunteer groups

(D) believes military families need more services

(E) thinks church affiliation supports recovery

6. The author mentions several cleaning products in paragraph 4 (lines 29-35) in order to

(A) illustrate how women search for easy ways to clean

(B) provide examples of cleaning aids that are safe to use

(C) inform the reader about toxic chemicals in the house

(D) explain how household detergents increase pollution

(E) provide evidence of products that leave an unhealthy residue

7. The author mentions presidential debates in paragraph 3 (lines 34-45) primarily to convey

(A) the persuasive power of debates

(B) the democratic process of electing a president

(C) the need to reach out to undecided voters in rural areas

(D) the need for direct confrontation between candidates

(E) the impact of "face-to-face" interaction on public perception

8. The first paragraph suggests that in the village

(A) no one works on religious holidays

(B) people attend church to catch up on local news

(C) people believe Sunday is a day of rest

(D) children engage in church-based recreation

(E) families organize community activities

9. George in Passage 2 and the narrator in Passage 1 are similar in that both

(A) think family heritage enhances opportunities

(B) share the same career aspirations

(C) feel driven to reach a higher standard of living

(D) desire the "perks" that come with a promotion

(E) feel uncertain about their financial future

10. In line 43, the "new political action" is best understood as a strategy to

(A) increase voter registration

(B) expand the use of absentee voting

(C) motivate young people to join a political party

(D) address the need for bipartisanship

(E) increase voter turnout on Election Day

Check the Answer Key on the next page.

ANSWER KEY
Shortcut #1: Speed Practice Drill C

Best Choices		Answer
1.	A or E	A
2.	B or D	D
3.	B or E	B
4.	B or D	B
5.	B or D	D
6.	B or E	E
7.	C or D	C
8.	B or C	C
9.	C or E	C
10.	A or E	E

SCORE BOX

Correct Answers	Raw Points	Scaled Points
1	1	10
2	2	20
3	3	30
4	4	40
5	5	50
6	6	60
7	7	70
8	8	80
9	9	90
10	10	100

_____ Your Total   _____ Your Raw Points   _____ Points Added to Your SAT Score!

Practice in Your SAT Workbooks

After completing the 3 Speed Practice Drills, you are the *all-seeing, all-knowing,* newly-minted **MASTER** of Shortcut #1. Now you can put it to work for you.

Go to any SAT workbook and scan the reading sections to see more examples of Shortcut #1. The more examples you see, the more this Shortcut will *stick* in your mind and pop out in the answer choices.

Nike tells you: *Just do it!*

Dr. Jay tells you: *Just use it!*

Just use it on every practice test you take, and you will be ready to snap up Shortcut #1 hidden inside your SAT test.

No Shortcut is Foolproof

Just as there are exceptions to every rule, you could possibly find an exception to **Shortcut #1**.

READING SHORTCUT #2

SECRET PATTERN:

2 ANSWER CHOICES that END with the SAME WORD(S):

(A) xxxxxxxxxxxxxxxxxxxxxxxx **reader**

(B) xxxxxxxxxxxxxxxx

(C) xxxxxxxxxxxxxxxxxxxxxxxxx

(D) xxxxxxxxxxxxxxxx

(E) xxxxxxxxxxxxxxxxxxxxxxxxx **reader**

Before you start to use the process of elimination (POE) to answer an SAT reading question or decide to skip a question, take *2 seconds* to scan the answer choices for this **secret pattern**: *2 answer choices that end with the same word(s).*

DETECT

2 answer choices (we'll call them X and Y) that end with the same word(s).

PREDICT

X or Y is the correct answer.

Rule out the other answer choices!

DECIDE

either X or Y.

If you are clueless, just pick X or Y. You **have a 50% chance** to select the correct answer – without thinking about either choice!

If you have a clue to tip your decision in favor of X or Y, you have a **much higher than 50% chance** to select the correct answer.

SCORE

| 1 correct answer | *gives you* | 1 (raw) point |
| 1 (raw) point | *roughly adds* | 10 points to your SAT score! |

The following 3 examples of Shortcut #2 are SNAPSHOTS that show you how extremely easy it is to recognize the **secret pattern** Shortcut #2 is based on: **2 answer choices end with the same word(s)**.

Example #1: BEFORE

Before you recognize the Shortcut, the SAT question is **difficult**. It is longer and harder to answer with 5 possible answers to read and think about.

1. It can be inferred from the passage that the author's parents were

   (A) disappointed in his behavior in school

   (B) out of touch with the demands of extra-curricular activities

   (C) unaware of how much bullying goes on in school

   (D) sensitive to the peer pressure he experienced

   (E) unavailable to help him manage homework

Example #1: AFTER

After you recognize the Shortcut, the question is **simple**. It is shorter and easier to answer with only 2 possible answers to read and think about.

1. It can be inferred from the passage that the author's parents were

   (A) disappointed by the author's poor grades `in school`
   (C) unaware of how much bullying goes on `in school`

In 2 seconds, Shortcut #2 turns HARD questions you SKIPPED on your last SAT test into EASY questions you can answer on your next SAT test!

Before you start to use the process of elimination (POE) to answer an SAT reading question or decide to skip a question, take **2 seconds** to scan the answer choices for this **secret pattern**: *2 answer choices that end with the same word(s).*

DETECT

"in school" in (A) and (C).

PREDICT

(A) or (C) is the correct answer.
Rule out the other answer choices!

DECIDE

either (A) or (C).

When you are totally clueless, just pick (A) or (C).
By the law of chance, you get a **great 50% chance** to select the correct answer.

When you have a clue to tip your decision in favor of (A) or (C), go for it.
By using a bit of knowledge, you get a **much higher than 50% chance** to select the correct answer.

SCORE

| 1 correct answer | *gives you* | 1(raw) point |
| 1 (raw) point | *roughly adds* | 10 points to your SAT score! |

Example #2: BEFORE

Before you recognize the Shortcut, the SAT question is **difficult**. It is longer and harder to answer with 5 possible answers to read and think about.

2. Lines 23-41 primarily encourage readers to view illness as

   (A) a cause for serious depression
   (B) a cruel part of the aging process
   (C) a catalyst for personal change
   (D) an external force for behavioral change
   (E) an opportunity for families to unite

Example #2: AFTER

After you recognize the Shortcut, the question is **simple**. It is shorter and easier to answer with only 2 possible answers to read and think about.

2. Lines 23-41 primarily encourage readers to view illness as

   (C) a catalyst for personal `change`
   (D) an external force for behavioral `change`

Before you start to use the process of elimination (POE) to answer an SAT reading question or decide to skip a question, take *2 seconds* to scan the answer choices for this **secret pattern:** *2 answer choices that end with the same word(s).*

DETECT

"change" in (C) and (D).

PREDICT

(C) or (D) is the correct answer.
Rule out the other answer choices!

DECIDE

either (C) or (D).

When you are totally clueless, just pick (C) or (D).
By the law of chance, you get a **great 50% chance** to select the correct answer.

When you have a clue to tip your decision in favor of (C) or (D), go for it.
By using a bit of knowledge, you get a **much higher than 50% chance** to select the correct answer.

SCORE

1 correct answer	*gives you*	**1(raw) point**
1 (raw) point	*roughly adds*	**10 points to your SAT score!**

Example #3: BEFORE

Before you recognize the Shortcut, the SAT question is **difficult**. It is longer and harder to answer with 5 possible answers to read and think about.

3. The second paragraph of the passage implies that the narrator felt

    (A) apprehensive about returning to his hometown
    (B) superior towards friends in his hometown
    (C) out of place in the old neighborhood
    (D) disoriented by new roads in the subdivision
    (E) glad he moved his family to a big city

Example #3: AFTER

After you recognize the Shortcut, the question is **simple**. It is shorter and easier to answer with only 2 possible answers to read and think about.

3. The second paragraph of the passage implies that the narrator felt

    (A) apprehensive about returning to his hometown
    (B) superior towards friends in his hometown

Before you start to use the process of elimination (POE) to answer an SAT reading question or decide to skip a question, take **2 seconds** to scan the answer choices for this **secret pattern**: *2 answer choices that end with the same word(s).*

DETECT

"his hometown" in (A) and (B).

PREDICT

(A) or (B) is the correct answer.

Rule out the other answer choices!

DECIDE

either (A) or (B).

When you are totally clueless, just pick (A) or (B).
By the law of chance, you get a **great 50% chance** to select the correct answer.

When you have a clue to tip your decision in favor of (A) or (B), go for it.
By using a bit of knowledge, you get a **much higher than 50% chance** to select the correct answer.

SCORE

1 correct answer	*gives you*	1(raw) point
1 (raw) point	*roughly adds*	**10 points to your SAT score!**

The POWER of KNOWING How to Analyze Answer Choices

After seeing Shortcut #2, you have the power of knowing exactly which **secret pattern** to look for in the answer choices that will give you an instant opportunity to score you never recognized before in SAT questions.

Shortcut #2: Speed Practice Drills

Now it is time to practice using Shortcut #2 to access opportunities to score on your SAT in *2 seconds – as fast as you click on Google or tap an app on your smartphone*. The questions in the drills are designed to develop your ability to rapidly scan the answer choices to detect this Shortcut to the correct answer: *the same word(s) at the end of 2 answer choices*.

The repetition built into the 3 drills will make scanning the answer choices for Shortcut #2 a part of your test-taking routine – a new habit to SCORE FAST. The faster you can snap up Shortcut #2 in the following drills, the better prepared you will be to take advantage of this Shortcut on your SAT test.

Shortcut #2: Speed Practice Drill A

1. In the second paragraph (lines 14-31) the reference to pets primarily serves to

    (A) point out that animal play is similar to child play

    (B) provide a way to teach children responsibility

    (C) expand upon the value of a home companion

    (D) call attention to the popularity of certain pets

    (E) elaborate on the role of house pets

2. The grandmother refers to "Somalia" (line 40) to impress upon the narrator that

    (A) immigrants are homesick in America

    (B) jobs in hotels did not exist in Somalia

    (C) natives have to adjust to living in a city

    (D) life was harder but simpler in Somalia

    (E) women in other countries are servants

3. The author of Passage 1 would most likely regard lines 57-62 in Passage 2 as evidence of the

    (A) lack of interest in reading the classics

    (B) range of nonfiction books in libraries

    (C) emergence of new categories of fiction

    (D) uneven quality of graphic novels

    (E) popularity of Japanese graphic novels

4. In lines 28-36, the narrator primarily conveys that pilgrims

    (A) yearned for a simpler way of life

    (B) felt alienated from their motherland

    (C) valued freedom above the comforts of home

    (D) found strength through meditation

    (E) united to protect their new home

5. Paragraph 2 (lines 31-47) is best described as an

(A) expansion of the author's observation

(B) exception to a widely held principle

(C) identification of a new element in a theory

(D) explanation of a popular theory

(E) analysis of a flaw in the design of the study

6. The question posed by the author in paragraph 2 serves to

(A) connect insomnia with writer's block

(B) expand on the need for holistic treatments

(C) propose a psychological cause for writer's block

(D) discredit the value of home remedies

(E) suggest that isolation leads to depression

7. It can be inferred from the passage that the narrator was

(A) concerned about parent expectations

(B) aware of the impact of time pressure

(C) encouraged by past academic performance

(D) realistic in setting college goals

(E) invested in maximizing student performance

8. The passage indicates that the early development of drugs to treat illnesses may have been delayed by

(A) lack of awareness of mind-body interactions

(B) limited knowledge of the origin of disease

(C) evidence collected primarily from sick animals

(D) inconclusive research on the causes of disease

(E) a disregard for the psychological effects of illness

9. The community event described in paragraph 3 would most effectively be promoted through

(A) church announcements

(B) fundraising brochures

(C) recreation center calendars

(D) community outreach newsletters

(E) local radio announcements

10. The narrator mentions that anyone who has not taken a cruise would be "surprised" (line 26) by the

(A) amount of food served on the ship

(B) differences in the size of the cabins

(C) number of people who get seasick

(D) range of activities off the ship

(E) concept of non-stop entertainment

Check the Answer Key on the next page.

ANSWER KEY
Shortcut #2: Speed Practice Drill A

	Best Choices	Answer
1.	D or E	E
2.	B or D	D
3.	D or E	D
4.	C or E	C
5.	C or D	C
6.	A or C	A
7.	C or E	E
8.	B or D	B
9.	A or E	A
10.	A or D	A

SCORE BOX

Correct Answers	Raw Points	Scaled Points
1	1	10
2	2	20
3	3	30
4	4	40
5	5	50
6	6	60
7	7	70
8	8	80
9	9	90
10	10	100

_____ Your Total   _____ Your Raw Points   _____ Points Added to Your SAT Score!

Shortcut #2: Speed Practice Drill B

1. In lines 66-69, the grandparent's response primarily indicates

   (A) a sympathetic approach to a dilemma

   (B) an acknowledgment of an awkward departure

   (C) an effort to help the children cope with separation

   (D) concern about the effect of the parent's decision

   (E) a sense of helplessness about the departure

2. The author of Passage 1 would most likely regard the phenomena described in lines 1-6 in Passage 2 as

   (A) an observation worthy of serious investigation

   (B) an event that adds to the mystery of *The Last Supper*

   (C) an incident that raises eyebrows among art collectors

   (D) a coincidence that enhances the value of *The Last Supper*

   (E) a common occurrence blown out of proportion

3. The last sentence of the first paragraph (lines 16-18) is intended to express the

   (A) impact of social networking

   (B) meaning of global connectivity

   (C) media's interest in new forms of networking

   (D) power of technology to create relationships

   (E) evolution in communicating online

4. The author mentions "activism" in line 13 in order to

   (A) explain the success of grassroots activities

   (B) suggest why door-to-door campaigning works

   (C) expose the influence of local commercials

   (D) indicate how television advertising is effective

   (E) question the usefulness of last-minute activities

5. Throughout Passage 1, the author seeks primarily to convey

   (A) delight in finding old photos of his grandparents
   (B) uncertainty about travelling alone
   (C) apprehension about tracking down ancestors
   (D) a desire to see where his family originated
   (E) anticipation associated with meeting ancestors

6. In lines 47-48 of Passage 2, the reference to "a void" suggests that

   (A) every man is an island separate from society
   (B) a person is responsible for himself
   (C) relationships are open-ended in society
   (D) human beings were not meant to live alone
   (E) man is a naturally social animal

7. The last paragraph of both passages primarily serves to

   (A) draw a conclusion based on historical findings
   (B) establish the artistic value of the sculpture
   (C) inform the reader about the artist's inherited collection
   (D) raise a question about the authenticity of the sculpture
   (E) offer a suggestion for future gallery events

8. In the third paragraph the narrator implies that he was

   (A) lonely travelling without his dog
   (B) uncomfortable sleeping in a tent with strangers
   (C) proud he reached camp first
   (D) glad he brought extra supplies
   (E) anxious to learn more about the strangers

9. The author's conclusion is most directly supported by the information concerning

   (A) which professional occupations limit leisure time
   (B) how people allocate their free time
   (C) the range of recreational opportunities
   (D) the level of expertise required in organized sports
   (E) the weekly commitment of different activities

10. Lines 33-51 primarily encourages readers to view sleep deprivation as

   (A) a cause of attention deficit disorder in children
   (B) an issue that requires lifestyle adjustments
   (C) a reminder of a basic human need
   (D) a problem that affects performance in school
   (E) a factor that contributes to obesity in children

Check the Answer Key on the next page.

ANSWER KEY
Shortcut #2: Speed Practice Drill B

Best Choices	Answer
1. B or E	B
2. B or D	D
3. A or C	A
4. A or E	E
5. C or E	C
6. A or C	C
7. B or D	D
8. B or E	B
9. A or B	A
10. A or E	E

SCORE BOX

Correct Answers	Raw Points	Scaled Points
1	1	10
2	2	20
3	3	30
4	4	40
5	5	50
6	6	60
7	7	70
8	8	80
9	9	90
10	10	100

_____ Your Total   _____ Your Raw Points   _____ Points Added to Your SAT Score!

Shortcut #2: Speed Practice Drill C

1. The author's remarks in lines 14-23 indicate that she views romance as a

   (A) natural part of a new courtship

   (B) prerequisite for a happy relationship

   (C) desirable element in a relationship

   (D) random occurrence among couples

   (E) sentimental idea that is not realistic

2. The author suggests that a blood sample (line 32) is necessary to

   (A) provide clear and convincing evidence

   (B) prevent the sentencing of innocent people

   (C) guard against the misinterpretation of evidence

   (D) support the accuracy of eyewitness testimony

   (E) ensure the conviction of criminals

3. In lines 12-17, the author primarily conveys that the students

   (A) hoped to see their friends in the half-time show

   (B) expected a band to start off the half-time show

   (C) had little enthusiasm for folk dancing

   (D) preferred live entertainment to a video performance

   (E) intended to dance after the lights were dimmed

4. According to the speaker in Passage 2, the "silence" (line 80) of the school board members indicated

   (A) opposition to the parent's proposal

   (B) an unwillingness to fund any proposal

   (C) a reluctance to continue the discussion

   (D) impatience with the statement of half-truths

   (E) disagreement with the request for a pilot study

5. The author describes "a girl in a newsroom" (line 7-12) in order to

   (A) expose the discrimination against women in journalism
   (B) portray herself as an innocent reporter
   (C) describe a battle to gain credibility in the newsroom
   (D) call attention to obstacles to success in journalism
   (E) point out differences in professional status

6. Which of the following statements about a suburban lifestyle is supported by both passages?

   (A) commuting adds time and stress to the work day
   (B) neighborhood schools foster a sense of belonging
   (C) church-based groups enhance suburban life
   (D) parks and recreation centers enhance the quality of life
   (E) larger homes contribute to migration to the suburbs

7. Which aspect of the film is of great concern to the critic in Passage 1 but is not mentioned by the critic in Passage 2?

   (A) violence in the opening scenes
   (B) negative chemistry between the characters
   (C) confusing use of flashbacks throughout a film
   (D) constant use of foul language
   (E) the triumph of evil in adult films

8. According to the narrator, in paragraph four, a crucial difference between family homes on the East Coast and on the West Coast is the

   (A) number of garages
   (B) location of the family room
   (C) typical additions to the property
   (D) amount of natural light inside the house
   (E) size of the dining room

9. Both the authors of Passage 1 and Passage 2 assume that the public is

   (A) immune to exaggerated statements made by the press
   (B) well-informed about their legal rights
   (C) indifferent to political corruption charges
   (D) concerned about ethical behavior in the courtroom
   (E) willing to be interviewed by the press

10. In passage 2, ESPN (line 51) is portrayed as a sports channel that

    (A) attracts a wide range of fans
    (B) broadcasts talk shows that appeal mostly to men
    (C) covers more teams than any other channel
    (D) combines entertainment with sports reporting
    (E) provides colorful pre-game reporting

Check the Answer Key on the next page.

ANSWER KEY
Shortcut #2: Speed Practice Drill C

	Best Choices	Answer
1.	B or C	C
2.	A or C	A
3.	A or B	A
4.	A or B	B
5.	A or D	D
6.	C or D	C
7.	C or E	C*
8.	B or E	E
9.	A or E	A
10.	D or E	D

SCORE BOX

Correct Answers	Raw Points	Scaled Points
1	1	10
2	2	20
3	3	30
4	4	40
5	5	50
6	6	60
7	7	70
8	8	80
9	9	90
10	10	100

_____ Your Total   _____ Your Raw Points   _____ Points Added to Your SAT Score!

* (Note that "film" and "films" are singular and plural versions of the same word. This is close enough to a match!)

Practice in Your SAT Workbooks

After completing the 3 Speed Practice Drills, you are the *all-seeing, all-knowing,* newly-minted **MASTER** of Shortcut #2. Now you can put it to work for you.

Go to any SAT workbook and scan the reading sections to see more examples of Shortcut #2. The more examples you see, the more this Shortcut will *stick* in your mind and pop out at you in your practice tests.

Nike tells you: *Just do it!*

Dr. Jay tells you: *Just use it!*

Just use it on every practice test you take, and you will be ready to snap up Shortcut #2 hidden inside your SAT test.

No Shortcut is Foolproof

Just as there are exceptions to every rule, you could possibly find an exception to **Shortcut #2.**

READING SHORTCUT #3

SECRET PATTERN:

2 ANSWER CHOICES that have the SAME WORD(S) in DIFFERENT PLACES:

(A) xxxxxxxxxxxxxxxxxxxxxxxxxx

(B) xxxxxxx**author**xxxxxxxxx

(C) xxxxxxxxxxxxxxxxxxxxxxxxx

(D) xxxxxxxxxxxxxxxx

(E) xxxx**author**xxxxxxxxxxxxxxxxxxxxxxxx

Before you start to use the process of elimination (POE) to answer an SAT reading question or decide to skip a question, take *2 seconds* to look for this **secret pattern**: *2 answer choices that have the same word(s) in different places.*

DETECT

2 answer choices (we'll call them X and Y) have the same word(s) in different places.

PREDICT

X or Y is the correct answer.

Rule out the other answer choices!

DECIDE

either X or Y.

If you are clueless, just pick X or Y. You **have a 50% chance** to select the correct answer – without thinking about either choice!

If you have a clue to tip your decision in favor of X or Y, you have a **much higher than 50% chance** to select the correct answer.

SCORE

1 correct answer	*gives you*	1 (raw) point
1 (raw) point	*roughly adds*	10 points to your SAT score!

The following 3 examples of Shortcut #3 are SNAPSHOTS that show you how extremely easy it is to recognize the **secret pattern** Shortcut #3 is based on: <u>**2 answer choices that have the same word(s) in different places.**</u>

Example #1: BEFORE

Before you recognize the Shortcut, the SAT question is **difficult**. It is longer and harder to answer with 5 possible answers to read and think about.

1. The exchange between the narrator and the airport security officer (lines 25-47) is best described as

   (A) an argument over the personality characteristics of leaders
   (B) a debate over the fairness of criteria used in developing ethnic labels
   (C) a discussion of the rules of survival in a gang culture
   (D) an attempt to defend the use of ethnic labels in law enforcement
   (E) a dialogue about individual vs. group profiles

Example #1: AFTER

After you recognize the Shortcut, the question is **simple**. It is shorter and easier to answer with only 2 possible answers to read and think about.

1. The exchange between the narrator and the airport security officer (lines 25-47) is best described as

    (B) a debate over the fairness of criteria used in developing ethnic labels

    (D) an attempt to defend the use of ethnic labels in law enforcement

In 2 seconds, Shortcut #3 turns HARD questions you SKIPPED on your <u>last SAT</u> test into EASY questions <u>you can answer</u> on your <u>next SAT test</u>!

Before you start to use the process of elimination (POE) to answer an SAT reading question or decide to skip a question, take *2 seconds* to scan the answer choices or this **secret pattern**: *2 answer choices that have the same word(s) in different places.*

DETECT

"ethnic labels" in (B) and (D).

PREDICT

(B) or (D) is the correct answer.

Rule out the other answer choices!

DECIDE

either (B) or (D).

When you are totally clueless, just pick (B) or (D).

By the law of chance, you get a **great 50% chance** to select the correct answer.

When you have a clue to tip your decision in favor of (B) or (D), go for it.

By using a bit of knowledge, you get a **much higher than 50% chance** to select the correct answer.

SCORE

| 1 correct answer | *gives you* | 1 (raw) point |
| 1 (raw) point | *roughly adds* | 10 points to your SAT score! |

Example #2: BEFORE

Before you recognize the Shortcut, the SAT question is **difficult**. It is longer and harder to answer with 5 possible answers to read and think about.

2. The mother refers to "Columbia " (line 64) to impress upon the reader her

    (A) pride in her homeland
    (B) desire to live near people from Columbia
    (C) struggle to find a good job in America
    (D) preference for a more productive life
    (E) success in Columbia as a businesswoman

Example #2: AFTER

After you recognize the Shortcut, the question is **simple**. It is shorter and easier to answer with only 2 possible answers to read and think about.

2. The mother refers to "Columbia " (line 64) to impress upon the reader her

    (B) desire to live near people from **Columbia**
    (E) success in **Columbia** as a businesswoman

Before you start to use the process of elimination (POE) to answer an SAT reading question or decide to skip a question, take *2 seconds* to scan the answer choices for this **secret pattern**: *2 answer choices that have the same word(s) in different places.*

DETECT

"Columbia" in (B) and (E).

PREDICT

(B) or (E) is the correct answer.

Rule out the other answer choices!

DECIDE

either (B) or (E).

When you are totally clueless, just pick (B) or (E).

By the law of chance, you get a **great 50% chance** to select the correct answer.

When you have a clue to tip your decision in favor of (B) or (E), go for it.

By using a bit of knowledge, you get a **much higher than 50% chance** to select the correct answer.

SCORE

| 1 correct answer | *gives you* | 1 (raw) point |
| 1 (raw) point | *roughly adds* | 10 points to your SAT score! |

Example #3: BEFORE

Before you recognize the Shortcut, the SAT question is **difficult**. It is longer and harder to answer with 5 possible answers to read and think about.

3. The author of Passage 2 implies that the "fossils" uncovered through the excavation (lines 36-39) are

   (A) evidence the archeologist's theory is accurate
   (B) likely to be contested by other geologists
   (C) similar to those found on a nearby island
   (D) essential information for developing a new theory
   (E) critical to funding the expansion of the excavation

Example #3: AFTER

After you recognize the Shortcut, the question is **simple**. It is shorter and easier to answer with only 2 possible answers to read and think about.

3. The author of Passage 2 implies that the "fossils" uncovered through the excavation (lines 36-39) are

   (A) evidence the archeologist's **theory** is accurate
   (D) essential information for developing a new **theory**

Before you start to use the process of elimination (POE) to answer an SAT reading question or decide to skip a question, take *2 seconds* to scan the answer choices for this **secret pattern**: *2 answer choices that have the same word(s) in different places.*

DETECT

"**theory**" in **(A)** and **(D)**.

PREDICT

(A) or (D) is the correct answer.

Rule out the other answer choices!

DECIDE

either (A) or (D).

When you are totally clueless, just pick (A) or (D).
By the law of chance, you get a **great 50% chance** to select the correct answer.

When you have a clue to tip your decision in favor of (A) or (D), go for it.
By using a bit of knowledge, you get a **much higher than 50% chance** to select the correct answer.

SCORE

| 1 correct answer | *gives you* | 1(raw) point |
| 1 (raw) point | *roughly adds* | 10 points to your SAT score! |

The POWER of KNOWING How to Analyze Answer Choices

After seeing Shortcut #3, you have the power of knowing exactly which **secret pattern** to look for in the answer choices that will give you an instant opportunity to score you never recognized before in SAT questions.

Shortcut #3: Speed Practice Drills

Now it is time to practice using Shortcut #3 to access opportunities to score on your SAT in *2 seconds – as fast as you click on Google or tap an app on your smartphone.* The questions in the drills are designed to develop your ability to rapidly scan the answer choices to detect this Shortcut to the correct answer: *the same word(s) in different locations in 2 answer choices.*

The repetition built into these 3 Speed Practice Drills will make scanning the answer choices for Shortcut #3 a part of your test-taking routine – a new habit to SCORE FAST. The faster you can snap up Shortcut #3 in the following drills, the better prepared you will be to take advantage of this Shortcut on your SAT test.

Shortcut #3: Speed Practice Drill A

1. The historian's purpose in lines 8-14 is to

   (A) advance a religious interpretation of events

   (B) elevate the importance of religious scholars

   (C) acknowledge several decades of progress

   (D) present an historical perspective on the issue

   (E) comment on the persistence of cultural bias

2. The two passages differ in that, Author 1

   (A) valued earning a high school diploma

   (B) viewed computer technology as his future

   (C) overcame his negative attitude toward math

   (D) found vocational school rewarding

   (E) stopped procrastinating and started working

3. The author of Passage 1 discusses flat screen televisions (line 65-76) in order to

   (A) argue that flat screens are affordable

   (B) predict that viewing a film at home will replace going to the movies

   (C) contrast the features of computers and televisions

   (D) claim that sporting events are best viewed on a flat screen

   (E) suggest that LCD is the wave of the future

4. In lines 9-11, the reference to the dog trainer suggests that dogs

   (A) have distinctly different personalities

   (B) communicate with their trainer

   (C) are sensitive to their trainer's voice

   (D) continue to be man's best friend

   (E) respond instantly to a range of commands

5. Lines 18-27 suggest that the author believes

(A) quilting is an artistic hobby

(B) starting a quilt shop requires unique skills

(C) the popularity of quilt shops is seasonal

(D) wool blankets are a practical alternative

(E) retired women are a captive market for sewing classes

6. The author uses golfing and tennis as examples (line 15-17) in order to primarily

(A) acknowledge that participation is expensive

(B) point out that recreational sports are also social events

(C) show their growing popularity among retired women

(D) associate both sports with country clubs

(E) emphasize the health benefits of physical activity

7. The authors of both passages would most likely agree that black women shared a

(A) keen awareness of slavery in world history

(B) fearlessness in the face of danger

(C) belief in the power of female role models

(D) determination to obtain equal rights

(E) desire for freedom from slavery

8. In lines 9-10, the narrator refers to "yesterday's rose" primarily in order to

(A) define the actress as outdated in her thinking

(B) portray the actress as out of touch with fashion

(C) suggest that appearance matters at every age

(D) comment on the value of investing in a wardrobe

(E) support the use of dress codes in the workplace

9. The author would most likely agree with which of the following statements

(A) children require close supervision around swimming pools

(B) swimming pools are dangerous for all age groups

(C) safety concerns outweigh creative play opportunities

(D) resale advantages outnumber the disadvantages

(E) maintenance and insurance costs are prohibitive

10. The statement in lines 20-23 suggests the narrator of Passage 1 believes that

(A) writing is essentially thinking on paper

(B) outlining is the key to organization

(C) editing is part of the composing experience

(D) proofreading increases the quality of an essay

(E) the five paragraph essay is overrated in America

Check the Answer Key on the next page.

ANSWER KEY
Shortcut #3: Speed Practice Drill A

Best Choices	Answer
1. A or B	B
2. A or D	A
3. A or D	D*
4. B or C	C*
5. B or C	C*
6. B or D	B
7. A or E	E
8. A or B	B
9. A or B	A
10. D or E	D

SCORE BOX

Correct Answers	Raw Points	Scaled Points
1	1	10
2	2	20
3	3	30
4	4	40
5	5	50
6	6	60
7	7	70
8	8	80
9	9	90
10	10	100

_____ Your Total   _____ Your Raw Points   _____ Points Added to Your SAT Score!

---

* (Note that these answers contain singular and plural versions of the same word. This is close enough to a match!)

Directions:

⏩ Set your timer or timer app for 40 seconds.

⏩ Underline the same word(s) in different locations in 2 answer choices in each question.

⏩ Circle 1 answer choice — without thinking about either choice.

Experience the awesome 50/50 chance you get to score a point the second you spot this Shortcut in the following questions.

1. The author mentions the "baseball team banners" (line 34) primarily in order to

   (A) praise the concept of parent donations

   (B) showcase how parents can work effectively with a coach

   (C) illustrate the impact of a small gift on team spirit

   (D) prove small gestures have a big benefit

   (E) promote the use of banners to show school pride

2. Mr. William's question (line 23), is most likely intended to

   (A) assess the support of his audience

   (B) focus the group's thinking on an issue

   (C) challenge his audience to take action

   (D) raise doubt about a popular proposal

   (E) encourage opposing points of view

3. The "secret" referred to in line 47 concerns the grandfather's

   (A) lack of medical insurance

   (B) chronic disability

   (C) unhealthy eating habits

   (D) unpaid medical bills

   (E) loss of unemployment benefits

4. Advocates of the proposal might best respond to the criticism in lines 37-44 by pointing out that the author

   (A) qualifies the results of his most recent study

   (B) has extensive experience conducting field research

   (C) draws upon established findings to validate his results

   (D) acknowledges the need to expand the sample size

   (E) recently received national recognition for his work

5. The authors of both passages recognize the value of

   (A) role playing

   (B) stimulating the imagination

   (C) playing house

   (D) sharing toys

   (E) modeling social behavior

6. The author's parenthetical aside in line 32 serves to

   (A) express sympathy for single mothers

   (B) question the purpose of the program

   (C) suggest the need for a support group

   (D) inject a different point of view

   (E) offer a reason to increase program funding

7. In lines 24-25, the term "fading" refers to the fact that the narrator

   (A) felt himself slipping into depression

   (B) had health issues that depleted his energy

   (C) easily become bored when left alone

   (D) realized he needed to reach out to friends

   (E) thought his friends tired of his company

8. In the context of the passage, Joe's first impression of Mary in lines 46-54 functions to emphasize his

   (A) social networking skill

   (B) attraction to girls who are athletes

   (C) bias toward meeting cheerleaders

   (D) interest in the most popular girls

   (E) belief that first impressions are lasting

9. The author of Passage 2 would most likely argue that the description of "how to give a speech" in Passage 1

   (A) overlooks the importance of rehearsing

   (B) downplays the need to incorporate examples

   (C) stresses clarity over being engaging

   (D) does not emphasize the importance of eye contact

   (E) values substance more than appearance

10. The "pep rally" (line 52-57) is best understood as an attempt to

   (A) show support for the football team

   (B) encourage teachers to attend tournaments

   (C) create an opportunity to build school spirit

   (D) increase student participation in athletic events

   (E) improve student interaction across grade levels

Check the Answer Key on the next page.

Best Choices	Answer
1. A or B	B
2. A or C	C
3. A or D	D
4. A or C	C
5. A or C	C
6. B or E	E
7. D or E	D
8. B or D	B
9. A or D	A
10. D or E	E

SCORE BOX

Correct Answers	Raw Points	Scaled Points
1	1	10
2	2	20
3	3	30
4	4	40
5	5	50
6	6	60
7	7	70
8	8	80
9	9	90
10	10	100

_____ Your Total   _____ Your Raw Points   _____ Points Added to Your SAT Score!

Shortcut #3: Speed Practice Drill C

1. The questions in lines 79-109 serve to

   (A) support the conclusion that adequate sleep prolongs life
   (B) argue that knowledge of sleep disorders is inadequate
   (C) point out that research using human subjects is limited
   (D) raise concerns about the effect of prolonged wakefulness
   (E) provide an example of a successful treatment program

2. The dialogue in lines 24-42 between Bobbie and her sister highlights

   (A) a common interest in physical fitness
   (B) how they encourage each other to excel
   (C) a natural rivalry between siblings
   (D) differences in their lifestyle
   (E) their equally competitive nature

3. The comparison of the salaries of movie stars and football players (lines 17-26) is cited in order to

   (A) portray both as celebrities
   (B) propose that their salaries are excessive
   (C) describe them as equally talented
   (D) suggest they both live in a bubble
   (E) argue for setting contract limits

4. According to lines 30-35, one reason to work part-time is to

   (A) save money for college
   (B) learn how to manage time
   (C) appreciate how hard parents work
   (D) think twice before spending money
   (E) become a more responsible young adult

5. The author's description of her plan to go back to India (lines 7-10) suggests that she

   (A) missed her servants and social status
   (B) was lonely living in New York City
   (C) wished she could speak better English
   (D) found New York City to be too expensive
   (E) regretted her job did not pay a higher salary

6. In lines 9-12 the author suggests that the teenagers were eager to dance because they

   (A) recognized their favorite songs
   (B) liked performing on a stage
   (C) enjoyed dancing with their friends
   (D) were bored sitting with adults
   (E) wanted to show their friends a new dance

7. In lines 43-48, the narrator mentions he is a physical therapist primarily to

   (A) emphasize his knowledge of the physical skeleton
   (B) suggest he is familiar with many physical ailments
   (C) establish that pain management is his specialty
   (D) convey that his time for volunteer work is limited
   (E) dispel any doubt about his role on the team

8. The author of Passage 2 mentions cellphones and ebooks in lines 54-64 primarily in order to

   (A) call attention to the extensive use of technology in school
   (B) argue for controlling the time spent wired to gadgets
   (C) offer a personal example of addiction
   (D) encourage face-to-face conversation
   (E) suggest that technology is redefining social interaction

9. The summers Carol and Jim were camp counselors is mentioned in lines 38-47 in order to

   (A) make the point that Carol was Jim's girlfriend
   (B) indicate their relationship evolved over many years
   (C) suggest Jim was first attracted to Carol in college
   (D) emphasize a common interest in counseling teenagers
   (E) portray them as role models for high school students

10. The question in lines 12-16 chiefly serves to

   (A) reinforce the role of a balanced diet in maintaining good health
   (B) focus attention on unhealthy eating habits
   (C) introduce a healthy approach to weight loss
   (D) raise awareness of the mind-body connection
   (E) encourage incorporating exercise into a healthy lifestyle

Check the Answer Key on the next page.

Best Choices	Answer
1. A or B	A
2. D or E	D
3. A or D	A
4. A or D	D
5. B or D	B*
6. C or E	C
7. A or B	B
8. A or E	E
9. A or C	C
10. C or E	E

SCORE BOX

Correct Answers	Raw Points	Scaled Points
1	1	10
2	2	20
3	3	30
4	4	40
5	5	50
6	6	60
7	7	70
8	8	80
9	9	90
10	10	100

_____ Your Total _____ Your Raw Points _____ Points Added to Your SAT Score!

* (While A and E both use the word "her," B and D use "New York City" which is a stronger match!)

Practice in Your SAT Workbooks

After completing the 3 Speed Practice Drills, you are the ***all-seeing, all-knowing,*** newly-minted **MASTER** of Shortcut #3. Now you can put it to work for you.

Go to any SAT workbook and scan the reading sections to see more examples of Shortcut #3. The more examples you see, the more this Shortcut will ***stick*** in your mind and pop out at you in your practice tests.

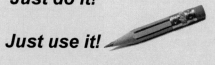

Nike tells you:	***Just do it!***
Dr. Jay tells you:	***Just use it!***

Just use it on every practice test you take, and you will be ready to snap up Shortcut #3 hidden inside your SAT test.

Mixed Reading Shortcut Speed Practice Drill: Shortcuts #1, 2 and 3

Now that you have learned Shortcuts #1, #2, and #3, it is time for a mixed review for you to practice seeing the same words in the answer choices in different locations. The Speed Practice Drill will help you develop speed and accuracy in your ability to snap up these Shortcuts in 2 seconds. Remember to follow the steps you have learned when answering the questions.

No Shortcut is Foolproof

Just as there are exceptions to every rule, you could possibly find an exception to **Shortcut #3**.

Mixed Speed Practice Drill:
Shortcut #1, #2, and #3

Directions:

▶▶ Set your timer or timer app for 2 minutes.

▶▶ Underline: instances of Shortcut #1 (*same word(s) at the beginning*), Shortcut #2 (*same word(s) at the end*), and Shortcut #3 (*same word(s) in different locations*) in 6 seconds or less. Some Shortcuts will pop out at you in 2 seconds, other may take a few more seconds.

▶▶ Circle 1 answer choice—without thinking about it.

Experience the awesome 50/50 chance you get to score a point the second you spot Shortcuts in the following questions.

---

1. The passage suggests that the narrator considers the discussion between the two men as

   (A) an attempt to avoid an argument

   (B) an example of the need to resolve differences

   (C) a conversation without any real consequences

   (D) the result of unresolved issues between friends

   (E) necessary because of ethnic differences

2. Mr. Jones's remarks in lines 58-67 is best described as

   (A) an acknowledgment of conflicting feelings

   (B) advice for a meaningful relationship

   (C) a forecast of a long, happy marriage

   (D) advice for achieving mutual understanding

   (E) an admission of his failure to communicate

3. The episode presented in Passage 1 is best described as a(n)

   (A) illustration of a dysfunctional family

   (B) demonstration of hostility between siblings

   (C) confrontation between parents from different cultures

   (D) collaboration between two like-minded adults

   (E) discussion about understanding in a family

4. In Passage 1, the "distinction" (line 15) refers to a difference between

   (A) the narrator's rehearsal and his live performance

   (B) the number of tickets available and actually sold

   (C) the reported and real size of the audience

   (D) the anticipated and actual hits on Twitter

   (E) the reviews of the matinee and evening performance

---

5. According to the narrator, the "deadlock" (line 40) indicates the jury's

(A) inability to find fault with an abused child

(B) different religious points of view

(C) preoccupation with the violence in the videotape

(D) inability to sort out conflicting emotions

(E) disagreement about the cause of the crime

6. On which of the following points would the authors of both passages most likely agree?

(A) hostile actions are not compatible with peaceful goals

(B) danger always exists for a hostile takeover

(C) social change is a slow and difficult process

(D) compromise is better than bloodshed

(E) small victories unify the supporters of a movement

7. The ad for "energy" water (lines 44-47) is cited as an example of the way marketing campaigns

(A) promote beverages as status symbols

(B) get consumers to buy products they do not need

(C) sell an expensive product with a superman image

(D) get endorsements from celebrities

(E) develop a brand that conveys an athletic image

8. The teenager's punishment was applauded by the community (lines 23-27) because they

(A) wanted to teach the boy a lesson

(B) regarded the boy as a neighborhood bully

(C) wanted the boy to serve as an example to others

(D) thought the boy's behavior was overlooked for too long

(E) believed punishment changes behavior

9. In creating an impression of the countryside, the author of Passage 2 makes use of

(A) expansive, rural images

(B) unique geographical features

(C) light and dark images

(D) plants and animal wildlife

(E) remote village landscapes

10. In lines 24-29, the inclusion of the musician's remarks is intended to

(A) call attention to an innovation in music

(B) demystify the image surrounding the individual

(C) provide insight into the group's use of technology

(D) connect the lyrics with the songwriter

(E) perpetuate the image of a musical genius

11. The imagery used in Passage 1 to market SUVs (lines 40-45) is intended to

(A) convey a feeling of safety to women

(B) spark a desire to take a road trip

(C) trigger a sense of power and control to men

(D) connect the vehicle with the rugged outdoors

(E) convey a sense of freedom and independence

12. The talk show host responds to the question posed in lines 34-35 by

(A) downplaying rumors he might leave the show

(B) disagreeing with the media's statement

(C) declining to answer any more questions

(D) restating how much he enjoys the show

(E) denying any conflict with the co-host

13. As used in lines 90-91, the "immediate challenge" refers to

(A) making a commitment to a goal

(B) dealing with obstacles to success

(C) confronting difficult alternatives

(D) putting forth extensive personal effort

(E) striving over time to achieve a goal

14. The author of Passage 2 uses the term "unjust" (line 3) in order to

(A) discourage further unjustifiable behavior

(B) advocate against the use of violence

(C) point out that the rule of law should prevail

(D) blame his enemies for overlooking previous crimes

(E) denounce seeking revenge after a crime is committed

15. The lawyer in Passage 1 and the narrator of Passage 2 are similar in that both are

(A) determined to help people rebuild their homes after the hurricane

(B) willing to provide their neighbors with legal advice

(C) inspired by friends on Facebook to volunteer

(D) committed to a long, slow recovery process

(E) investing time and money in restoring homes

16. The author's main point about "body language" (line 12-14) is that it

(A) cannot easily be controlled by the individual

(B) provokes different responses from individuals

(C) has a powerful impact on social interaction

(D) carries universally understood messages

(E) transcends different cultural norms

17. In lines 23-26 the physician advises the author to

(A) focus on managing, not fixing the problem

(B) develop a comprehensive exercise routine

(C) monitor pain levels between sessions

(D) attend physical therapy twice a week

(E) report any new symptoms between sessions

18. The author describes himself as "primarily left-handed" (line 6-9) in order to

(A) reveal that he is ambidextrous

(B) suggest he has unique abilities

(C) illustrate he has made adaptions

(D) suggest he has overcome a handicap

(E) invite speculation about his flexibility

19. The author uses cooking and cleaning as examples (line 15- 18) primarily in order to

(A) acknowledge that domestic tasks can be labor intensive

(B) suggest that maintaining a home is a never-ending job

(C) interject the popularity of new apps for household chores

(D) suggest the need for couples to share responsibilities

(E) propose that the benefits of a housekeeper may be worth the cost

20. The second paragraph of the passage implies that the narrator felt

(A) out of place in a rural hospital

(B) concerned about the quality of care

(C) out of place among elderly patients

(D) worried about the doctor's diagnosis

(E) relieved surgery was not necessary

Check the Answer Key on the next page.

ANSWER KEY
Mixed Reading Speed Practice Drill: Shortcut #1, 2 and 3

Shortcut Used	Best Choices	Answer	Shortcut Used	Best Choices	Answer
1. Shortcut 2	B or E	E	11. Shortcut 1	A or E	A
2. Shortcut 1	B or D	B	12. Shortcut 2	A or D	D
3. Shortcut 2	A or E	A	13. Shortcut 2	A or E	A
4. Shortcut 2	A or E	E	14. Shortcut 3	D or E	D
5. Shortcut 1	A or D	A	15. Shortcut 3	A or E	E
6. Shortcut 3	A or B	B	16. Shortcut 2	A or B	B
7. Shortcut 2	C or E	C	17. Shortcut 2	C or E	C
8. Shortcut 3	D or E	D	18. Shortcut 1	B or D	B
9. Shortcut 2	A or C	C	19. Shortcut 1	B or D	D
10. Shortcut 3	B or E	E	20. Shortcut 1	A or C	C

SCORE BOX

Correct Answers	Raw Points	Scaled Points	Correct Answers	Raw Points	Scaled Points
1	1	10	11	11	110
2	2	20	12	12	120
3	3	30	13	13	130
4	4	40	14	14	140
5	5	50	15	15	150
6	6	60	16	16	160
7	7	70	17	17	170
8	8	80	18	18	180
9	9	90	19	19	190
10	10	100	20	20	200
___ Your Total	___ Your Raw Points	____ Points Added to Your SAT Score!	___ Your Total	___ Your Raw Points	____ Points Added to Your SAT Score!

READING SHORTCUT #4

RULE WHEN <u>a word(s) in the Introduction to a passage matches a word(s) in 1 answer choice</u>, THEN the 1 choice that follows this **secret pattern** is the best answer.

SECRET PATTERN:

SAME WORD(S) in the INTRODUCTION and in 1 ANSWER CHOICE:

Introduction: xxxxxxxxxxxxxxxxxxxxxx
charity xxxxxxxxxxxxxxxxxxxxxxxxxxxx

(A) xxxxxxxxxxxxxxxxxxxxxxxxxxxxxx
(B) xxx**charity**xxxxxxxxxxxxxxxxxxxxx
(C) xxxxxxxxxxxxxxxxxxxxxxxxxxxxxx
(D) xxxxxxxxxxxxxxxxxxxxxxxxxxxxxx
(E) xxxxxxxxxxxxxxxxxxxxxxxxxxxxxx

REWARD The instant you RECOGNIZE this secret pattern you get the POWER to SCORE on the SAT <u>without thinking about any of the answer choices!</u>

You can predict (B) is the CORRECT ANSWER.

Before you start to use the process of elimination (POE) to answer an SAT reading question or decide to skip a question, take *2 seconds* to look for this **secret pattern**: *the same word(s) in the Introduction to the passage and in 1 answer choice.*

DETECT

the same word(s) in the Introduction and in 1 answer choice (we'll call it X).

PREDICT

X is the correct answer.

Rule out the other answer choices!

DECIDE

X.

Just pick X. You have a **near 100% chance** to select the correct answer – without thinking about the choice!

If you have a clue to tip your decision in favor of X, you can be almost certain X is the correct answer.

SCORE

| **1 correct answer** | *gives you* | **1 (raw) point** |
| **1 (raw) point** | *roughly adds* | **10 points to your SAT score!** |

The following 3 examples of Shortcut #4 are SNAPSHOTS that show you how extremely easy it is to recognize the **secret pattern** Shortcut #4 is based on: **a word(s) in the italicized Introduction matches a word(s) in 1 answer choice.**

Example #1: BEFORE

Before you recognize the Shortcut, the SAT question is **difficult**. It is longer and harder to answer with 5 possible answers to read and think about.

Introduction: *In the following passage the author offers his views on the relationship between hard work and success.*

1. The primary purpose of this passage is to

   (A) show the impact of parenting on academic achievement
   (B) discuss efforts to embrace the American Dream
   (C) highlight cultural differences between communities
   (D) emphasize the significance of the relationship
   (E) support the idea that it takes a village to raise a child

Example #1: AFTER

After you recognize the Shortcut, the question is **simple**. It is shorter and easier to answer with only 1 possible answer to read and think about.

Introduction: *In the following passage the author offers his views on the* **relationship** *between opportunity and hard work.*

    1. The primary purpose of this passage is to

       (D) emphasize the significance of the **relationship**

In 2 seconds, Shortcut #4 turns HARD questions you SKIPPED on your last SAT test into EASY questions you can answer on your next SAT test!

Before you start to use the process of elimination (POE) to answer an SAT reading question or decide to skip a question, take *2 seconds* to scan the answer choices for this **secret pattern**: *the same word(s) in the Introduction to the passage and in 1 answer choice.*

DETECT

"relationship" in the Introduction and in (D).

PREDICT

(D) is the correct answer.
Rule out the other answer choices!

DECIDE

(D).

Just pick (D). You get a **near 100% chance** to select the correct answer.

When you have a clue to tip your decision in favor of (D), go for it. By using a bit of knowledge, you can be almost certain (D) is the correct answer.

SCORE

| 1 correct answer | *gives you* | 1(raw) point |
| 1 (raw) point | *roughly adds* | **10 points to your SAT score!** |

Example #2: BEFORE

Before you recognize the Shortcut, the SAT question is **difficult**. It is longer and harder to answer with 5 possible answers to read and think about.

Introduction: *This passage was adapted from a 1997 book about life on other planets.*

2. The primary purpose of the passage is to

   (A) point out the conflicting research findings
   (B) put forth evidence of extra-terrestrial life
   (C) argue for funding planetary research
   (D) explain different theories about life on other planets
   (E) dispel the mystery associated with outer space

Example #2: AFTER

After you recognize the Shortcut, the question is **simple**. It is shorter and easier to answer with only 1 possible answer to read and think about.

Introduction: *This passage was adapted from a 1997 book about life on other planets.*

2. The primary purpose of the passage is to

   (D) Explain different theories about life on other planets

Before you start to use the process of elimination (POE) to answer an SAT reading question or decide to skip a question, take *2 seconds* to scan the answer choices for this **secret pattern**: *the same word(s) in the Introduction to the passage and in 1 answer choice.*

DETECT

"life on other planets" in the Introduction and in (D).

PREDICT

(D) is the correct answer.

Rule out the other answer choices!

DECIDE

(D).

Just pick (D). You get a **near 100% chance** to select the correct answer.

When you have a clue to tip your decision in favor of (D), go for it. By using a bit of knowledge, you can be almost certain (D) is the correct answer.

SCORE

1 correct answer	*gives you*	1 (raw) point
1 (raw) point	*roughly adds*	10 points to your SAT score!

Example #3: BEFORE

Before you recognize the Shortcut, the SAT question is **difficult**. It is longer and harder to answer with 5 possible answers to read and think about.

Introduction: *In this excerpt from a short story, Karen faces a decision whether or not to divorce her husband.*

3. The purpose of this passage is to

    (A) detail the events leading up to a decision
    (B) explain the deterioration in a relationship
    (C) relate how a spouse was once a thoughtful person
    (D) reveal the inner thoughts of a unhappy, married woman
    (E) explore the interpersonal dynamics of a marriage

Example #3: AFTER

After you recognize the Shortcut, the question is **simple**. It is shorter and easier to answer with only 1 possible answer to read and think about.

Introduction: *In this excerpt from a short story, Karen faces a* **decision** *whether or not to divorce her husband.*

3. The purpose of the passage is to

    (A) detail the events leading up to her **decision**

STRATEGY

Before you start to use the process of elimination (POE) to answer an SAT reading question or decide to skip a question, take *2 seconds* to scan the answer choices for this **secret pattern**: *the same word(s) in the Introduction to the passage and in 1 answer choice.*

DETECT

"decision" in the Introduction and in (A).

PREDICT

(A) is the correct answer.

Rule out the other answer choices!

DECIDE

(A).

Just pick (A). You still get a **near 100% chance** to select the correct answer.

When you have a clue to tip your decision in favor of (A), go for it. By using a bit of knowledge, you can be almost certain (A) is the correct answer.

SCORE

| 1 correct answer | *gives you* | 1 (raw) point |
| 1 (raw) point | *roughly adds* | **10 points to your SAT score!** |

The POWER of KNOWING How to Analyze Answer Choices

After seeing Shortcut #4, you have the power of knowing exactly which **secret pattern** to look for in the answer choices that will give you an instant opportunity to score you never recognized before in SAT questions.

Shortcut #4: Speed Practice Drills

Now it is time to practice using Shortcut #4 to access opportunities to score on your SAT in *2 seconds – as fast as you click on Google or tap an app on your smartphone.* The questions in the drills are designed to develop your ability to rapidly scan the answer choices to detect this Shortcut to the correct answer: *a word(s) in the italicized introduction matches a word(s) in 1 answer choice.*

The repetition built into the 3 drills will make scanning the answer choices for Shortcut #4 a part of your test-taking routine – a new habit to SCORE FAST. The faster you can snap up Shortcut #4 in the following drills, the better prepared you will be to take advantage of this Shortcut on your SAT test.

Shortcut #4: Speed Practice Drill A

Directions:

▶▶ Set your timer or timer app for 60 seconds.

▶▶ Underline the word(s) in the Introduction that match the word(s) in 1 answer choice.

▶▶ Circle 1 answer choice — without thinking about it.

Experience the awesome near 100% chance you get to score a point the second you spot this Shortcut in the following questions.

1. Introduction: *The following is adapted from an article about people who suffer from dementia.*
   The primary purpose of this passage is to
   (A) explain the impact of memory loss on daily life
   (B) describe the stages of a debilitating disease
   (C) explain the safety issues associated with mental deterioration
   (D) educate family members about the effects of dementia
   (E) present a classic case study of an elderly man

2. Introduction: *This passage is adapted from the introduction to a textbook about economic instability.*
   The primary purpose of the passage is to show how the author
   (A) created an international model for analyzing financial data
   (B) promoted fiscal conservatism through a series of conferences
   (C) conducted research on trends in emerging financial markets
   (D) became an expert on forecasting downturns in the economy

   (E) developed a textbook based on case studies of economic instability

3. Introduction: *The following passage is from a novel about a girl who is reunited with a long-lost cousin.*
   The statement that best captures the purpose of this passage is a
   (A) reunion with a distant relative
   (B) homecoming between members of the same cast
   (C) heartwarming discovery of a long-lost cousin
   (D) chance encounter with a forgotten family member
   (E) journey recapturing a childhood memory

4. Introduction: *The passage below discusses a ground-breaking discovery in the treatment of heart disease.*
   The author's primary purpose in the passage is to
   (A) present a new approach to treating heart disease
   (B) elaborate on the benefits of a new drug
   (C) discuss the need to verify the research findings

(D) explain the significance of a large sample size

(E) suggest a promising alternative to surgery

5. Introduction: *The following is an excerpt from a speech on the negative impact of cellphones in the classroom given by a high school principal.*

Cellphones are viewed as

(A) distracting students from learning

(B) encouraging a new form of cheating

(C) creating an unfair advantage for some students

(D) causing an increase in copying homework

(E) contributing to discipline problems in classrooms

6. Introduction: *This passage is from a book about the art of reflection.*

The passage is best described as

(A) a definition of a thoughtful process

(B) an example of a relaxation technique

(C) a discussion of the value of daily reflection

(D) a description of a healthy mental habit

(E) a lesson in maintaining good mental health

7. Introduction: *The following passage considers the reliability of procedures used in psychological evaluations.*

The primary purpose of the passage is to

(A) raise concerns about how mental illness is diagnosed

(B) examine ambiguities in psychological evaluations

(C) shed light on cultural factors that influence assessment

(D) explain the meaning of "mentally competent" to stand trial

(E) examine problems associated with expert testimony

8. Introduction: *The following passage is from a commencement address delivered by an expert in forensic science.*

The primary purpose of the passage is to

(A) highlight the career path of an expert in forensic science

(B) recap inspiring anecdotes from a college graduation speech

(C) showcase how crime shows on T.V. mirror real police investigations

(D) outline major developments in a relatively new field of study

(E) inspire graduate students to research new uses for DNA evidence

9. Introduction: *This passage is adapted from an article about unhealthy ingredients in fast food.*

The primary purpose of the passage is to report on the

(A) confusion created by inaccurate advertising

(B) harmful effects of fried food

(C) consumption of "empty calories"

(D) difficulty in tracing ingredients in fast food

(E) leading cause of obesity in young children

10. Introduction: *The following passage is adapted from an article about the Martin Luther King, Jr. Memorial in Washington, D.C.*

The primary purpose of this passage is to

(A) describe the centerpiece of the monument

(B) educate tourists about the significance of this memorial

(C) connect the structure to the "I Have a Dream" speech

(D) explain how the inscription was selected

(E) clarify confusion surrounding the dedication ceremony

Check the Answer Key on the next page.

ANSWER KEY
Shortcut #4: Speed Practice Drill A

Answer
1. D
2. E
3. C
4. A
5. E
6. C
7. B
8. A
9. D
10. B

SCORE BOX

Correct Answers	Raw Points	Scaled Points
1	1	10
2	2	20
3	3	30
4	4	40
5	5	50
6	6	60
7	7	70
8	8	80
9	9	90
10	10	100

_____ Your Total   _____ Your Raw Points   _____ Points Added to Your SAT Score!

Shortcut #4: Speed Practice Drill B

1. Introduction: *The passage is from a young Immigrant girl's diary.*
   The primary purpose of the passage is to explain how the author
   - **(A)** became the first person in her family to go to college
   - **(B)** understood hard work to be essential to a better life
   - **(C)** discovered her career through an encounter with a fellow immigrant
   - **(D)** recognized technology as the key to her future in America
   - **(E)** successfully balanced work and night school

2. Introduction: *The following passage is from an essay discussing the decline in reading novels.*
   The purpose of the passage is to
   - **(A)** explain the shift in reading from the novel to short stories
   - **(B)** argue for more student choice in the selection of books
   - **(C)** critique the impact of technology on reading fiction
   - **(D)** call for rebalancing non-fiction and fiction requirements
   - **(E)** track changes in high school reading assignments

3. Introduction: *The following passage is taken from the introduction to a book about cooking with parchment paper.*
   The purpose of this passage is primarily to
   - **(A)** revolutionize the way food is prepared at home
   - **(B)** demonstrate how to treat mom to an easy parchment supper
   - **(C)** introduce a great Mother's Day present
   - **(D)** demonstrate how to cook without using a pot or pan
   - **(E)** offer quick and healthy suggestions for meals on the go

4. Introduction: *The following passage is taken from a book for college students about how to manage the demands of college life.*
   The primary purpose of this passage is to
   - **(A)** inspire students on how to maximize their academic success
   - **(B)** present examples of real-life situations students face
   - **(C)** introduce high school students to higher education
   - **(D)** help students transition from living at home to living on campus
   - **(E)** describe practical ways to balance the demands of college life

5. Introduction: *The following passage was adapted from an article about two violinists in a high school orchestra.*

The passage is best described as

(A) an introduction to a musician through the perspective of a peer

(B) a nostalgic depiction of the role of music in education

(C) a story of how two musicians inspired others to excel

(D) a tribute to the talent of two violinists in high school

(E) an illustration of an enduring friendship

6. Introduction: *This excerpt is from a memoir written by a teenage boy who emigrated from China to the United States.*

The passage primarily serves to

(A) provide a detailed account of a rewarding journey

(B) describe the hardships encountered in America

(C) reveal why young people migrated to the United States

(D) recount the heartache of separation from family

(E) chronicle the expectations of Chinese parents

7. Introduction: *The following passage is adapted from an essay on women and careers.*

The author of this passage is primarily concerned with the

(A) impact of working outside the home on family life

(B) tension between roles inside and outside the home

(C) challenges women face in the workplace

(D) career aspirations of married women

(E) need to balance working with caring for children

8. Introduction: *The following is from an article on the relationship between the fields of sociology and economics.*

The author's primary purpose is to

(A) pinpoint how two fields intersect in society

(B) recognize the contribution of both fields

(C) discuss how financial policy impacts society

(D) define economics and sociology as separate but equal

(E) explain how both disciplines affect prosperity

9. Introduction: *The following is adapted from a website that describes the history of the Apple computer.*

The primary purpose of the passage is to

(A) describe how the Apple computer changed the world

(B) provide a snapshot of innovation in the 21st century

(C) characterize Steve Jobs as a charismatic pioneer

(D) explain how the first laptop was developed

(E) highlight the early life of a technology wizard

10. Introduction: *The following is adapted from an article about a TV show called "The Franchise" that was based on the Florida Marlins baseball team.*

The author's primary purpose is to

(A) report real conflicts that fueled each episode of the show

(B) tell the story of how the Florida Marlins rebuilt their team

(C) highlight events throughout the season that appeared in the media

(D) convey the drama between the producer and the team manager

(E) capture the dynamic personalities of the baseball players on film

Check the Answer Key on the next page.

ANSWER KEY
Shortcut #4: Speed Practice Drill B

Answer
1. C
2. A*
3. B
4. E
5. D
6. C
7. D
8. D
9. A
10. B

SCORE BOX

Correct Answers	Raw Points	Scaled Points
1	1	10
2	2	20
3	3	30
4	4	40
5	5	50
6	6	60
7	7	70
8	8	80
9	9	90
10	10	100

_____ Your Total   ____ Your Raw Points   ____ Points Added to Your SAT Score!

---

* (This is another situation where you are matching a word and it's plural. This match is close enough!)

Shortcut #4: Speed Practice Drill C

Directions:

⏩ Set your timer or timer app for 30 seconds.

⏩ Underline the word(s) in the introductions to the passages that match the word(s) in the answer choices in each question.

⏩ Circle 1 answer choice — without thinking about it.

Experience the awesome near 100% chance you get to score a point the second you spot this Shortcut in the following questions.

1. Introduction: *The passage below is excerpted from a book about international relations.*
The primary purpose of the passage is to show how the author
(A) developed a global framework for trade agreements
(B) became an international ambassador for world peace
(C) introduced a new approach to negotiating peace talks
(D) integrated economic theory and diplomacy
(E) studied cultural barriers to economic reform

2. Introduction: *The following passages consider the relationship between literature and film.*
In contrast to the author of Passage 2, the author of Passage 1 is more concerned with the
(A) decline of dialogue in character development
(B) lack of aesthetic quality in movies made for television
(C) ways in which films contribute to the popular culture

(D) challenges of turning a bestselling novel into a blockbuster movie
(E) use of literary devices to entertain the audience

3. Introduction: *The following passage is from a novel about a man and his horse.*
The best description of this passage would be
(A) a reunion of a cowboy with his trusted companion
(B) a reminder of how animals add to the quality of life
(C) an example of taking on responsibility in life
(D) an emotional relationship with nature
(E) one man's journey through a challenging life

4. Introduction: *The following passage is from an essay that discusses the decline of good manners in American culture.*
The main purpose of the passage is to
(A) increase public awareness of rude behavior
(B) outline the causes for the decline in good manners

(C) call for new rules for a more civil society

(D) expose how technology disrupts conversations

(E) raise questions about appropriate social behavior

5. Introduction: *The following passage discusses the early stages of a women's career.*

The primary purpose of the passage is to show how the author

(A) dealt with the rejection of her ideas

(B) developed her marketing skills

(C) wrote a compelling business proposal

(D) adjusted her career aspirations

(E) expanded her professional network

6. Introduction: *The following is adapted from a biology textbook.*

This passage is primarily concerned with

(A) translating scientific terms into everyday language

(B) simplifying the study of abstract concepts in biology

(C) the value of observation in learning about science

(D) the role of labs in applying the scientific method

(E) the use of graphs and charts in analyzing data

7. Introduction: *The following passage chronicles the career of the Beatles.*

The primary purpose of the passage is to

(A) describe the major tours that launched the band

(B) chronicle the hit songs that made the Beatles famous

(C) explain John Lennon's contributions to the band's success

(D) demonstrate the impact of the band across the globe

(E) distinguish this group of musicians from all others

8. Introduction: *This passage, adapted from a newspaper article, discusses the movement known as Cubism.*

The primary purpose of the passage is to

(A) recognize Pablo Picasso as the inventor of a new art form.

(B) discuss the primitive characteristics of Cubist paintings

(C) explain how artists were guided by the work of Cezanne

(D) define the attitudes and intentions of a group of artists

(E) clarify the confusion surrounding the meaning of "Cubism"

9. Introduction: *The following passage is about family life in Greece.*

The primary purpose of the passage is to

(A) highlight the importance of religion in community life

(B) describe the domestic roles of Greek men and women

(C) compare family life in Greece with family life in America

(D) explain the social expectations of women in small towns

(E) detail how children are cared for by their parents

10. Introduction: *The following passages are taken from two articles in a magazine about intellectual property.*

The primary issue addressed in both passages is

(A) defining the types of properties protected

(B) protecting intellectual property from theft

(C) appealing to legal groups for protection

(D) closing common loopholes in copyright laws

(E) seeking compensation for copyright violations

Check the Answer Key on the next page.

ANSWER KEY
Shortcut #4: Speed Practice Drill C

Answer

1. B
2. C*
3. E*
4. B
5. D
6. B
7. B
8. E
9. C
10. B

SCORE BOX

Correct Answers	Raw Points	Scaled Points
1	1	10
2	2	20
3	3	30
4	4	40
5	5	50
6	6	60
7	7	70
8	8	80
9	9	90
10	10	100

_____ Your Total   _____ Your Raw Points   _____ Points Added to Your SAT Score!

* (The answers to questions 2 and 3 show you can match words that are plural or possessive versions of themselves. They are close enough for a match!)

Practice in Your SAT Workbooks

After completing the 3 Speed Practice Drills, you are the **all-seeing, all-knowing,** newly-minted **MASTER** of Shortcut #4. Now you can put it to work for you.

Go to any SAT workbook and scan the reading sections to see more examples of Shortcut #4. The more examples you see, the more this Shortcut will *stick* in your mind and pop out at you in your practice tests.

Nike tells you: *Just do it!*

Dr. Jay tells you: *Just use it!*

Just use it on every practice test you take, and you will be ready to snap up Shortcut #4 hidden inside your SAT test.

No Shortcut is Foolproof

Just as there are exceptions to every rule, you could possibly find an exception to **Shortcut #4**.

READING SHORTCUT #5

<table>
<tr>
<td>

RULE

</td>
<td>

This rule has 2 parts:

When **the tone of a passage is positive**, THEN 1 of the answer choices that contains a **positive word(s) is the correct answer**.

When the tone of a passage is negative, THEN 1 of the answer choices that contains a **negative word(s) is the correct answer**.

</td>
</tr>
</table>

SECRET PATTERN:

THE TONE of the PASSAGE MATCHES THE TONE of WORDS in the ANSWER CHOICES:

PASSAGE: xxxxxxxxxxxxxxxxxxxxxxxxxxxxxxxxxxxx
xxxxxxxxxx The tone of the passage is negative xxx
xxxxxxxxxxxxxxxxxxxxxxxxxxxxxxxxxxxxxxxxxxxxxxxxx.

(A) pessimistic x

(B) xxxxxxxxxxx

(C) xxxxxxxxxxx

(D) xxxxxxxxxxx

(E) antagonistic

<table>
<tr>
<td>

REWARD

</td>
<td>

The instant you RECOGNIZE this pattern you get the POWER to SCORE on the SAT without thinking about ALL 5 answer choices!

You can predict (A) or (E) is the CORRECT ANSWER.

</td>
</tr>
</table>

Before you start to use the process of elimination (POE) to answer an SAT reading question or decide to skip a question, take *2 seconds* to look for this **secret pattern**: *the correct answer matches the tone of the passage.*

Positive passages have 2 or 3 positive answer choices.

Negative passages have 2 or 3 negative answer choices.

DETECT

the tone of the passage and match it with the tone of some answer choices (we'll call them X, Y, and Z).

PREDICT

X, Y, or Z is the correct answer.

Rule out the other answer choices!

DECIDE

either X, Y, or Z.

If you are clueless, just pick X, Y or Z. You still **have a 33% chance** to select the correct answer – without thinking about the choices!

If you have a clue to tip your decision in favor of X, Y or Z, you have a **much higher than 33% chance** to select the correct answer.

SCORE

| 1 correct answer | *gives you* | 1 (raw) point |
| 1 (raw) point | *roughly adds* | 10 points to your SAT score! |

The following 3 examples of Shortcut #5 are SNAPSHOTS that show you how extremely easy it is to recognize the **secret pattern** Shortcut #5 is based on: <u>**the tone of the passage matches the tone of 2 or 3 answer choices.**</u>

Example #1: BEFORE

Before you recognize the Shortcut, the SAT question is **difficult**. It is longer and harder to answer with 5 possible answers to read and think about.

Passage: *The tone of the passage is negative.*

1. The author's attitude toward the protestors can best be described as

   (A) hostile
   (B) disapproving
   (C) tolerant
   (D) sympathetic
   (E) laudatory

Example #1: AFTER

After you recognize the Shortcut, the question is **simple**. It is shorter and easier to answer with only 2 possible answers to read and think about.

Passage: *The tone of the passage is negative.*

1. The author's attitude toward the protestors can best be described as

(A) hostile
(B) disapproving

In 2 seconds, Shortcut #5 turns HARD questions you SKIPPED on your last SAT test into EASY questions you can answer on your next SAT test!

STRATEGY

Before you start to use the process of elimination (POE) to answer an SAT reading question or decide to skip a question, take *2 seconds* to match the tone of a passage with the tone of words in the answer choices, scan the answer choices for this **secret pattern**:

the correct answer matches the tone of the passage.

DETECT

the negative tone in the passage and in answer choices (A) and (B).

PREDICT

(A) or (B) is the correct answer.
Rule out the other answer choices!

DECIDE

either (A) or (B).

When you are totally clueless, just pick (A) or (B).
By the law of chance, you get a **great 50% chance** to select the correct answer.

When you have a clue to tip your decision in favor of (A) or (B), go for it.
By using a bit of knowledge, you get a **much higher than 50% chance** to select the correct answer.

SCORE

| 1 correct answer | *gives you* | 1(raw) point |
| 1 (raw) point | *roughly adds* | 10 points to your SAT score! |

Example #2: BEFORE

Before you recognize the Shortcut, the SAT question is **difficult**. It is longer and harder to answer with 5 possible answers to read and think about.

Passage: *The tone of the passage is positive.*

2. The tone of the statement in lines 33-35 ("The reason... son) is best described as

   (A) optimistic
   (B) controversial
   (C) skeptical
   (D) condescending
   (E) enlightened

Example #2: AFTER

After you recognize the Shortcut, the question is **simple**. It is shorter and easier to answer with only 2 possible answers to read and think about.

Passage: *The tone of the passage is positive.*

2. The tone of the statement in lines 33-35 (The reason...son) is best described as:

   (A) optimistic
   (E) enlightened

STRATEGY

Before you start to use the process of elimination (POE) to answer an SAT reading question or decide to skip a question, take *2 seconds* to scan the answer choices for this **secret pattern**:

the correct answer matches the tone of the passage.

DETECT

the positive tone of the passage and in answer choices (A) and (E).

PREDICT

(A) or (E) is the correct answer.
Rule out the other answer choices!

DECIDE

either (A) or (E).

When you are totally clueless, just pick (A) or (E).
By the law of chance, you get a **great 50% chance** to select the correct answer.

When you have a clue to tip your decision in favor of (A) or (E), go for it.
By using a bit of knowledge, you get a **much higher than 50% chance** to select the correct answer.

SCORE

1 correct answer	*gives you*	1(raw) point
1 (raw) point	*roughly adds*	10 points to your SAT score!

Example #3: BEFORE

Before you recognize the Shortcut, the SAT question is **difficult**. It is longer and harder to answer with 5 possible answers to read and think about.

> Passage: *The tone of the passage is negative.*
>
> 3. The author's comments suggest that he regards the tour guide as
>
>   (A) idealistic
>   (B) jocular
>   (C) egotistical
>   (D) naïve
>   (E) supercilious

Example #3: AFTER

After you recognize the Shortcut, the question is **simple**. It is shorter and easier to answer with only 2 possible answers to read and think about.

> Passage: *The tone of the passage is negative.*
>
> 3. The author's comments suggest that he regards the tour guide as
>
>   (C) egotistical
>   (D) naïve
>   (E) supercilious

STRATEGY

Before you start to use the process of elimination (POE) to answer an SAT reading question or decide to skip a question, take *2 seconds* to scan the answer choices for this **secret pattern**:

the correct answer matches the tone of the passage.

DETECT

the negative tone in the passage and in answer choices (C), (D) and (E).

PREDICT

(C), (D), or (E) is the correct answer.
Rule out the other answer choices!

DECIDE

either (C), (D) or (E).

When you are totally clueless, just pick (C), (D), or (E). By the law of chance, you still **get a 33% chance** to select the correct answer.

When you have a clue to tip your decision in favor of (C), (D), or (E), go for it.
By using a bit of knowledge, you get a **much higher than 33% chance** to select the correct answer.

SCORE

1 correct answer	*gives you*	1(raw) point
1 (raw) point	*roughly adds*	10 points to your SAT score!

The POWER of KNOWING How to Analyze Answer Choices

After seeing Shortcut #5, you have the power of knowing exactly which **secret pattern** to look for in the answer choices that will give you an instant opportunity to score you never recognized before in SAT questions.

Shortcut #5: Speed Practice Drills

Now it is time to practice using Shortcut #5 to access opportunities to score on your SAT in *2 seconds – as fast as you click on Google or tap an app on your smartphone.* The questions in the drills are designed to develop your ability to rapidly scan the answer choices to detect this Shortcut: ***the correct answer matches the tone of the passage.***

The repetition built into the 3 drills will make scanning the answer choices for Shortcut #5 a part of your test-taking routine – a new habit to SCORE FAST. The faster you can snap up Shortcut #5 in the following drills, the better prepared you will be to take advantage of this Shortcut on your SAT test.

Shortcut #5: Speed Practice Drill A

The passage conveys a positive tone or feeling.

1. The author's attitude is best described as one of

    (A) annoyance
    (B) distrust
    (C) ambivalence
    (D) sincerity
    (E) optimism

The passage conveys a negative tone or feeling.

2. Which of the following best describes the author's tone in the last paragraph?

    (A) gloomy
    (B) skeptical
    (C) hopeful
    (D) satisfied
    (E) bland

The passage conveys a positive tone or feeling.

3. The author's attitude toward the "thinkers" (line 43) is best characterized as

    (A) supportive
    (B) innocuous
    (C) cautious
    (D) critical
    (E) practical

The passage conveys a negative tone or feeling.

4. The tone of the political discussion in lines 56-64 is best characterized as

    (A) instructive
    (B) balanced
    (C) enlightening
    (D) bombastic
    (E) partisan

5. In lines 28-30, the narrator suggests that Russell's tendency is to be

   (A) obstinate
   (B) cooperative
   (C) reasonable
   (D) conciliatory
   (E) didactic

The passage conveys a positive feeling or tone.

6. In lines 44-53, the author of Passage 1 offers an argument that is best defined as

   (A) plausible
   (B) unrealistic
   (C) laudable
   (D) unsettling
   (E) convincing

The passage conveys a negative feeling or tone.

7. In Passage 2, the author's position can best be described as

   (A) inaccurate
   (B) enthusiastic
   (C) misleading
   (D) instructive
   (E) contentious

The passage conveys a positive feeling or tone.

8. The author's response to the "green movement" (line 49) is best characterized as

   (A) apprehensive
   (B) pragmatic
   (C) optimistic
   (D) defensive
   (E) antiquated

The passage conveys a negative feeling or tone.

9. Rob's attitude toward the "real estate investment" is best described as

   (A) intrigued
   (B) cynical
   (C) enthusiastic
   (D) insightful
   (E) resentful

The passage conveys a positive feeling or tone.

10. In lines 5-10, Jim characterizes Alex's resume as

   (A) substantial
   (B) elementary
   (C) concise
   (D) lackluster
   (E) focused

Check the Answer Key on the next page.

Best Choices	Answer
1. D or E	D
2. A, B, or E	B
3. A or E	A
4. D or E	D
5. A or E	A
6. A, C, or E	C
7. A, C, or E	E
8. B or C	B
9. B or E	E
10. A, C, or E	C

SCORE BOX

Correct Answers	Raw Points	Scaled Points
1	1	10
2	2	20
3	3	30
4	4	40
5	5	50
6	6	60
7	7	70
8	8	80
9	9	90
10	10	100

_____ Your Total   _____ Your Raw Points   _____ Points Added to Your SAT Score!

Shortcut #5: Speed Practice Drill B

The passage conveys a positive feeling or tone.

1. The author of Passage 2 would most likely characterize the arguments made by the author of Passage 1 as

   (A) inconclusive

   (B) forward-thinking

   (C) narrow-minded

   (D) plausible

   (E) impractical

The passage conveys negative feeling or tone.

2. In lines 31-47 there is a shift in feelings from

   (A) fear to courage

   (B) concern to worry

   (C) doubt to certainty

   (D) disapproval to support

   (E) animated to resigned

(Note: Use the last word in each answer choice to identify the negative choices.)

The passage conveys a positive feeling or tone.

3. The author's attitude toward "children" in paragraph 3 can best be described as

   (A) compassionate

   (B) dismissive

   (C) benevolent

   (D) insensitive

   (E) protective

The passage conveys a positive feeling or tone.

4. In lines 2-31 the narrator suggests that Jerry's approach to resolving disputes tends to be

   (A) defensive

   (B) sarcastic

   (C) philosophical

   (D) altruistic

   (E) fair

The passage conveys a negative feeling or tone.

5. The author viewed "the mountain trail" (line 8) with

   (A) curiosity
   (B) apprehension
   (C) defiance
   (D) trepidation
   (E) enthusiasm

The passage conveys a negative feeling or tone.

6. The passage suggests that "most teenagers" go through a stage of

   (A) exuberance
   (B) rebellion
   (C) denial
   (D) withdrawal
   (E) insight

The passage conveys a positive feeling or tone.

7. The author's statement in the last paragraph is best described as

   (A) unsettling
   (B) realistic
   (C) impassive
   (D) conciliatory
   (E) reassuring

Passage 2 conveys a negative feeling or tone.

8. Compared to the tone in Passage 1, the tone in Passage 2 is more

   (A) open-minded
   (B) alarming
   (C) optimistic
   (D) argumentative
   (E) opinionated

The passage conveys a negative feeling or tone.

9. In lines 21-43, the author's attitude toward the new subway system is best described as

   (A) tolerant
   (B) reassuring
   (C) impassive
   (D) pragmatic
   (E) skeptical

The passage conveys a positive feeling or tone.

10. The discussion of airline safety in lines 34-56 is best characterized as

    (A) adversarial
    (B) compromising
    (C) judicious
    (D) pessimistic
    (E) prudent

Check the Answer Key on the next page.

ANSWER KEY
Shortcut #3: Speed Practice Drill B

	Best Choices	Answer
1.	B or D	D
2.	B or E	B
3.	A, C, or E	A
4.	C, D, or E	E
5.	B, C, or D	D
6.	B, C, or D	B
7.	B, D, or E	B
8.	B, D, or E	E
9.	C or E	C
10.	B, C, or E	C

SCORE BOX

Correct Answers	Raw Points	Scaled Points
1	1	10
2	2	20
3	3	30
4	4	40
5	5	50
6	6	60
7	7	70
8	8	80
9	9	90
10	10	100

_____ Your Total   _____ Your Raw Points   _____ Points Added to Your SAT Score!

Shortcut #5: Speed Practice Drill C

The passage conveys a negative feeling or tone.

1. In lines 41-52, the narrator suggests that energy bars are

    (A) nutritious
    (B) unhealthy
    (C) indigestible
    (D) practical
    (E) bland

The passage conveys a positive feeling or tone.

2. The last line of Passage 2 suggests that the author of Passage 1 is

    (A) idealistic
    (B) short-sighted
    (C) verbose
    (D) narcissistic
    (E) realistic

The passage conveys a positive feeling or tone.

3. In lines 23-45, the author of Passage 1 offers a perspective that is best defined as

    (A) dispassionate
    (B) sobering
    (C) affable
    (D) circuitous
    (E) energizing

The passage conveys a positive feeling or tone.

4. The discussion of the "nuclear power plant" in lines 41-56 is best characterized as

    (A) enlightening
    (B) explosive
    (C) patronizing
    (D) enervating
    (E) succinct

The passage conveys a negative feeling or tone.

5. In lines 13-22, the narrator suggests that the coach is sometimes

   (A) verbose
   (B) benevolent
   (C) punitive
   (D) humorous
   (E) cantankerous

The passage conveys a negative feeling or tone.

6. Which of the following best describes the author's tone in the third paragraph?

   (A) sympathetic
   (B) stubborn
   (C) suspicious
   (D) forgiving
   (E) dismissive

The passage conveys a positive feeling or tone.

7. The tone of the author's remarks about graphic novels might best be described as

   (A) critical
   (B) open-minded
   (C) antiquated
   (D) enthusiastic
   (E) tentative

The passage conveys a positive feeling or tone.

8. In line 23, "silent" most nearly means the audience is

   (A) focused
   (B) content
   (C) unresponsive
   (D) disapproving
   (E) engaged

Passage 2 conveys a positive feeling or tone.

9. Compared to the tone of Passage 1, the tone of Passage 2 is more

   (A) dogmatic
   (B) scholarly
   (C) exuberant
   (D) conciliatory
   (E) antagonistic

The passage conveys a negative feeling or tone.

10. The passage suggests that the narrator primarily viewed the text message as

   (A) humorous
   (B) amusing
   (C) annoying
   (D) boorish
   (E) clever

Check the Answer Key on the next page.

Best Choices	Answer
1. B, C, or E	B
2. A or E	A
3. C or E	C
4. A or E	E
5. A, C, or E	A
6. B, C, or E	E
7. B or D	D
8. A, B, or E	D
9. B, C, or D	C
10. C or D	D

SCORE BOX

Correct Answers	Raw Points	Scaled Points
1	1	10
2	2	20
3	3	30
4	4	40
5	5	50
6	6	60
7	7	70
8	8	80
9	9	90
10	10	100

_____ Your Total   _____ Your Raw Points   _____ Points Added to Your SAT Score!

Practice in Your SAT Workbooks

After completing the 3 practice drills, you are the ***all-seeing, all-knowing,*** newly-minted **MASTER** of Shortcut #5. This Shortcut just entered your SAT Toolbox. Now you can put it to work for you.

Go to any SAT workbook and scan the reading sections to see more examples of Shortcut #5. The more examples you see, the more this Shortcut will ***stick*** in your mind and pop out at you in the answer choices.

Nike tells you: *Just do it!*

Dr. Jay tells you: *Just use it!*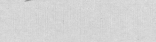

Just use it on every practice test you take, and you will be ready to snap up Shortcut #5 hidden inside your SAT test.

No Shortcut is Foolproof

Just as there are exceptions to every rule, you could possibly find an exception to **Shortcut #5**.

WRITING SHORTCUT #6

RULE — WHEN the words at the end of answer choice (A) match the words at the end of 1 other answer choice, THEN 1 of these 2 choices is the correct answer.

SECRET PATTERN:

The Words at the END OF ANSWER CHOICE (A) MATCH the WORDS at the END of 1 OTHER ANSWER CHOICE:

(A) xxxxxxxxxxxxxxx liked walking **over the bridge.**

(B) xxxxxxxxxxxxxxxxxxxxxxxxxxxxxxxxxxxxxxxxxxxx

(C) xxxxxxxxxxxx walked **over the bridge.**xxxxxxxxx

(D) xxxxxxxxxxxxxxxxxxxxxxxxxxxxxxxxxxxxxxxxxxx

(E) xxxxxxxxxxxxxxxxxxxxxxxxxxxxxxxxxxxxxxxxxxx

Scoring Bonus: The SAT does NOT like the "ing" form of verbs.

When 1 of the 2 answer choices contains a word that ends with **"ing,"** you can eliminate this choice and predict the remaining choice is the correct answer. In this example, you can eliminate answer choice (A) and predict (C) is the correct answer.

REWARD — The instant you RECOGNIZE this secret pattern you get the POWER to SCORE on the SAT without thinking about ALL 5 answer choices!

You can predict (A) or (C) is the CORRECT ANSWER.

Before you start to use the process of elimination (POE) to answer an SAT reading question or decide to skip question, take *2 seconds* to scan the answer choices for this **secret pattern**: *the words at the end of answer choice (A) match the words at the end of 1 other answer choice.*

DETECT

answer choice (A) ends with the same word(s) as 1 other answer choice (we'll call it X).

PREDICT

(A) or X is the correct answer.

Rule out the other answer choices!

DECIDE

either (A) or X.

If you are clueless, just pick (A) or X. You **have a 50% chance** to select the correct answer – without thinking about either choice!

If you have a clue like the "ing" Scoring Bonus to tip your decision in favor of (A) or X, you have a **much higher than 50% chance** to select the correct answer.

SCORE

| 1 correct answer | *gives you* | 1(raw) point |
| 1 (raw) point | *roughly adds* | 10 points to your SAT score! |

Writing Shortcut #6: EXAMPLES

The following 3 examples of Shortcut #6 are SNAPSHOTS that show you how extremely easy it is to recognize the simple pattern Shortcut #6 is based on: **the words at the end of answer choice (A) match the words at the end of 1 other answer choice.**

Example #1: BEFORE

Before you recognize the Shortcut, the SAT question is **difficult**. It is longer and harder to answer with 5 possible answers to read and think about.

1. Although the museum is open seven days a week, the guides conduct <u>tours only on weekends</u>.

    (A) the guides conduct tours only on weekends

    (B) the tour guides limit their tours to the weekends

    (C) the guides are conducting tours only on weekends

    (D) the guided tours are only available on weekends

    (E) the tour guides limit tours to weekends

Example #1: AFTER

After you recognize the Shortcut, the question is **simple**. It is shorter and easier to answer with only 2 possible answers to read and think about.

1. Although the museum is open seven days a week, the guides conduct tours only on weekends. Underline "tours only on weekends" in this question

    (A) the guides conduct tours only on weekends
    (C) the guides are conducting tours only on weekends

In 2 seconds, Shortcut #6 turns a hard question you skipped on your last SAT into an easy question you can answer on your next SAT.

Before you start to use the process of elimination (POE) to answer an SAT writing question or decide to skip a question, take *2 seconds* to scan the answer choices for this **secret pattern**: *the words at the end of answer choice (A) match the words at the end of 1 other answer choice.*

DETECT

"tours only on weekends" at the end of answer choices (A) and (C).

PREDICT

(A) or (C) is the correct answer.

Rule out the other answer choices!

DECIDE

(A) or (C).

When you are totally clueless, just pick (A) or (C).
By the law of chance, you get a **great 50% chance** to select the correct answer.

When you have a clue like the "ing" Scoring Bonus to tip your decision in favor of (A) or (C), go for it.
By using a bit of knowledge, you get a **much higher than 50% chance** to select the correct answer.

SCORE

| 1 correct answer | *gives you* | 1(raw) point |
| 1 (raw) point | *roughly adds* | 10 points to your SAT score! |

Before you recognize the Shortcut, the SAT question is **difficult**. It is longer and harder to answer with 5 possible answers to read and think about.

2. The committee charged with finding a new activities director wanted to find someone with high school experience, a great reputation, and <u>someone with an ability to inspire the coaches</u>.

(A) someone with an ability to inspire the coaches
(B) they wanted someone who could inspire coaches
(C) someone to inspire the coaches
(D) an ability to be able to inspire the coaches
(E) an ability to inspire the coaches

After you recognize the Shortcut, the question is **simple**. It is shorter and easier to answer with only 2 possible answers to read and think about.

2. The committee charged with finding a new activities director wanted to find someone with high school experience, a great reputation, and <u>someone with an ability to inspire the coaches</u>.

(A) someone with **an ability to inspire the coaches**
(E) **an ability to inspire the coaches**

Before you start to use the process of elimination (POE) to answer an SAT writing question or decide to skip a question, take *2 seconds* to scan the answer choices for this **secret pattern**: *the words at the end of answer choice (A) match the words at the end of 1 other answer choice.*

DETECT

"an ability to inspire the coaches" at the end of answer choices (A) and (E).

PREDICT

(A) or (E) is the correct answer.
Rule out the other answer choices!

DECIDE

either (A) or (E).

When you are totally clueless, just pick (A) or (E).
By the law of chance, you get a **great 50% chance** to select the correct answer.

When you have a clue like the "ing" Scoring Bonus to tip your decision in favor of (A) or (E), go for it.
By using a bit of knowledge, you get a **much higher than 50% chance** to select the correct answer.

SCORE

| 1 correct answer | *gives you* | 1(raw) point |
| 1 (raw) point | *roughly adds* | 10 points to your SAT score! |

Example #3: BEFORE

Before you recognize the Shortcut, the SAT question is **difficult**. It is longer and harder to answer with 5 possible answers to read and think about.

3. An internationally known singer who is able to change her style as she ages, <u>Celine Dion's songs always fit with the music of the time.</u>

   (A) Celine Dion's songs always fit with the music of the time.
   (B) the songs of Celine Dion always seem to fit into the time
   (C) Celine Dion sings songs that always fit with the music of the time
   (D) the music of the time always fits into Celine Deon's songs
   (E) Celine Dion always fits the music of the time with her songs.

Example #3: AFTER

After you recognize the Shortcut, the question is **simple**. It is shorter and easier to answer with only 2 possible answers to read and think about.

3. An internationally known singer who is able to change her style as she ages, <u>Celine Dion's songs always fit the music of the time.</u>

   (A) Celine Dion's songs **always fit with the music of the time**.
   (C) Celine Dion sings songs that **always fit with the music of the time**.

Before you start to use the process of elimination (POE) to answer an SAT writing question or decide to skip a question, take *2 seconds* to scan the answer choices for this **secret pattern**: *the words at the end of answer choice (A) match the words at the end of 1 other answer choice.*

DETECT

"always fits with the music of the time" at the end of answer choices (A) and (C).

PREDICT

(A) or (C) is the correct answer.
Rule out the other answer choices!

DECIDE

either (A) or (C).

When you are totally clueless, just pick (A) or (C).
By the law of chance, you get a **great 50% chance** to select the correct answer.

When you have a clue like the "ing" Scoring Bonus to tip your decision in favor of (A) or (C), go for it.
By using a bit of knowledge, you get a **much higher than 50% chance** to select the correct answer.

SCORE

| 1 correct answer | *gives you* | 1(raw) point |
| 1 (raw) point | *roughly adds* | 10 points to your SAT score! |

The POWER of KNOWING How to Analyze Answer Choices

After seeing Shortcut #6, you have the power of knowing exactly which **secret pattern** to look for in the answer choices that will give you an instant opportunity to score you never recognized before in SAT questions.

Shortcut #6: Speed Practice Drills

Now it is time to practice using Shortcut #6 to access opportunities to score on your SAT in *2 seconds – as fast as you click on Google or tap an app on your smartphone.* The questions in the drills are designed to develop your ability to rapidly scan the answer choices to detect this Shortcut to the correct answer: ***answer (A) ends with the same word(s) as 1 other answer choice.***

The repetition built into the 3 drills will make scanning the answer choices for Shortcut #6 a part of your test-taking routine – a new habit to SCORE FAST. The faster you can snap up Shortcut #6 in the following drills, the better prepared you will be to take advantage of this Shortcut on your SAT test.

Shortcut #6: Speed Practice Drill A

1. Above the garage door <u>there is a light fixture once inhabited by sparrows.</u>

   (A) there is a light fixture once inhabited by sparrows.
   (B) there are a light fixture once inhabited by sparrows.
   (C) there would be a light fixture where sparrows inhabited
   (D) a light fixture was once inhabited by some sparrows.
   (A) a light fixture was once inhabited with sparrows.

2. The men hiked miles to find <u>firewood, and returning before dusk</u> with over fifty pounds of firewood on their backs.

   (A) firewood, and returning before dusk
   (B) firewood, to be returning before the dusk
   (C) firewood, they returned before it was dusk
   (D) firewood and returned before dusk
   (E) firewood to have returned by dusk

3. The construction of the new school <u>was to have been completed in September, but</u> a delay in the delivery of student desks postponed the opening until October.

   (A) was to have been completed in September, but
   (B) was not completed in September, but will be
   (C) was to be completed in September, but
   (D) will have to be completed after September, but
   (E) were to be completed by September, but

4. When flat screen televisions first became <u>available at a lower price we wondered if it were defective.</u>

   (A) available at a lower price we wondered if it were defective
   (B) available at such a low price, we wondered if they were not defective
   (C) available at a low price we thought they could be defective
   (D) available at a low price we started to think they must be defective
   (E) available at a lower price, we wondered if they were defective

5. The two cars in the showroom were dissimilar enough to explain the differences in their sticker price.

   (A) to explain the differences in their sticker price

   (B) to explain their having different sticker prices

   (C) to explain the difference in their sticker price

   (D) to have prices that were different

   (E) to be having different sticker prices

6. New handheld devices will allow doctors to diagnose patients, and let them access patient records without leaving their homes.

   (A) let them access patient records without

   (B) access patient records with no need of

   (C) access patient's records and not be

   (D) to access patient records without ever

   (E) access patient records without

7. Many high school marching bands from around the country auditioned to participate in the Macy's Thanksgiving Day Parade, but only a few were selected.

   (A) but only a few were selected

   (B) but few were selected to participate

   (C) and a few were selected

   (D) and few were finally selected

   (E) but, however, only a few were selected.

8. Results of a recent poll indicates that voters thinking that family values are the first criteria in assessing the character of a politician.

   (A) thinking that family values are the first

   (B) think that family values can be the first

   (C) think that family value could be the first

   (D) think that family values are the first

   (E) think their family values should be the first

9. Some universities have a three-year degree program, which offer financial advantages to students and their families.

   (A) program, which offer financial advantages to students and

   (B) program, which offers financial advantages to students and

   (C) program which offer financial advantages to students plus

   (D) program; to offer financial advantages to students as well as

   (E) program to offer financial advantages for students and

10. To attract more customers on Valentine's Day, the school leadership committee sold its flowers cheaply to everyone in the lunchroom.

   (A) sold its flowers cheaply

   (B) sold their flowers cheaply

   (C) will sell cheap flowers

   (D) priced their flowers to sell

   (E) will sell flowers at a low price

Check the Answer Key on the next page.

ANSWER KEY
Shortcut #6: Speed Practice Drill A

Best Choices	Answer
1. A or B	A
2. A or D	D – *use "ing" clue to rule out A*
3. A or C	C
4. A or E	E
5. A or C	C
6. A or E	E
7. A or E	A
8. A or D	D – *use "ing" clue to rule out A*
9. A or B	B
10. A or B	B

SCORE BOX

Correct Answers	Raw Points	Scaled Points
1	1	10
2	2	20
3	3	30
4	4	40
5	5	50
6	6	60
7	7	70
8	8	80
9	9	90
10	10	100

_____ Your Total   _____ Your Raw Points   _____ Points Added to Your SAT Score!

Shortcut #6: Speed Practice Drill B

Directions:

▶▶ Set your timer or timer app for 40 seconds.

▶▶ Underline the answer choice that ends the same as answer choice (A) in each question.

▶▶ Check for words that end in "ing" to get a Shortcut Bonus.

▶▶ Circle 1 answer choice — without thinking about either choice.

Experience the awesome 50/50 chance you get to score a point the second you spot this Shortcut in the following questions.

1. The English teacher's book collection, is the largest in the English Department.

   (A) collection, is the largest in the English Department
   (B) collection is larger than the English Department collection
   (C) collection is the largest in the English Department
   (D) collection is larger than the English Departments
   (E) collection; it is the largest in the English Department

2. While shopping online for a prom dress, that was when Caroline decided to go to the factory outlet.

   (A) dress, that was when Caroline decided to go to the factory outlet
   (B) dress, Caroline decided to go to the factory outlet mall
   (C) dress, then Caroline's decision was to go to the factory outlet
   (D) dress, going to the factory outlet was Caroline's decision
   (E) dress, Caroline made the decision to go to the factory outlet

3. New cellphone rules requires students to leave their cellphones in their lockers until school is dismissed.

   (A) requires students to leave their cellphones
   (B) requiring students leave their cellphones
   (C) require leaving cellphones in lockers
   (D) require students to leave their cellphones
   (E) are requiring students leave cellphones

4. The coach selected Alex to be the pinch hitter in the baseball game, since his batting average was better than either one, Bill or Bob.

   (A) either one, Bill or Bob
   (B) either Bill or else Bob
   (C) either Bill or that of Bob
   (D) that of Bill and of Bob
   (E) either Bill or Bob

5. When everyone was in the auditorium for the holiday show, <u>that was the time that the computers were stolen from the classrooms</u>.

    (A) that was the time that the computers were stolen from the classrooms

    (B) the computers were stolen from the classrooms

    (C) at this time, computers were stolen from classrooms

    (D) then the computers were stolen from some of the classrooms

    (E) then was the time the computers in the classrooms were stolen

6. Because the train was non-stop, <u>they slept for a number of hours</u>.

    (A) they slept for a number of hours

    (B) therefore sleep was possibly for hours

    (C) sleeping was possible for a number of hours

    (D) they went to sleep for hours on the train

    (E) therefore for a number of hours they slept

7. Although the museum is open seven days a week, <u>the guides conduct tours only on weekends</u>.

    (A) the guides conduct tours only on weekends

    (B) the tour guides are limiting their tours to the weekends

    (C) the guides are conducting tours only on weekends

    (D) the guides will be conducting their tours on weekends

    (E) the tour guides limit the tours on the weekend

8. A police officer was sent out to investigate <u>a neighbor's claim that a</u> teenager stole a motorcycle from his driveway.

    (A) a neighbor's claim that

    (B) a neighbor with a claim that

    (C) a neighbor who was claiming that

    (D) that a neighbor claimed

    (E) a claim made by a neighbor that

9. Performing a card trick, like any skill, <u>requiring many hours of practice</u> before it becomes easy.

    (A) requiring many hours of practice

    (B) requires many hours of practice

    (C) requiring, among other things, hours of practice

    (D) requires that you practice for many hours

    (E) requires continuous practice

10. Mary volunteered to make coffee for the ceremony, not wanting to be the one <u>that had to clean up after everyone went home</u>.

    (A) that had to clean up after everyone went home

    (B) that was there when everyone went home

    (C) who had to clean up after everyone went home

    (D) who was there when the ceremony ended

    (E) that was left with a chore after the ceremony

Check the Answer Key on the next page.

ANSWER KEY
Shortcut #6: Speed Practice Drill B

Best Choices	Answer
1. A or C	C
2. A or B	B
3. A or D	D
4. A or E	E
5. A or B	B
6. A or C	A – *use "ing" to rule out C*
7. A or C	A – *use "ing" to rule out C*
8. A or B	A
9. A or B	B – *use "ing" to rule out A*
10. A or C	C

SCORE BOX

Correct Answers	Raw Points	Scaled Points
1	1	10
2	2	20
3	3	30
4	4	40
5	5	50
6	6	60
7	7	70
8	8	80
9	9	90
10	10	100

_____ Your Total   _____ Your Raw Points   _____ Points Added to Your SAT Score!

Shortcut #6: Speed Practice Drill C

1. High school students have the opportunity to choose from a variety of electives, some may be related to a future college major.

   (A) electives, some may be related
   (B) electives, some may be relating
   (C) electives; each may be relating
   (D) electives; each of which relates
   (E) electives, one of many may be related

2. Carrying the groceries up to the eighth floor, fatigue caused Gary to stop and take a break for a minute.

   (A) fatigue caused Gary to stop and take a break
   (B) fatigue is what caused Gary to stop and take a break
   (C) it was fatigue that caused Gary to stop
   (D) Gary, fatigued, stopped and took a break
   (E) Gary, fatigued, stopped to take a break

3. There are a long list of symptoms for the common cold, including hoarseness, cough, watery eyes, headache, fatigue, and fever.

   (A) There are a long list of symptoms for the common cold,
   (B) There were long lists of symptoms for common colds,
   (C) There is a long list of symptoms for the common cold,
   (D) There is a long list of the symptoms for every type of cold;
   (E) Their are symptoms for common colds,

4. Without analyzing the question, you cannot expect that you will achieve a high grade on the exam.

   (A) you cannot expect that you will achieve a high grade on the exam
   (B) you cannot expect your achievement to be a high grade
   (C) your high grade cannot be achieved on the exam
   (D) you cannot expect to achieve a high grade on the exam
   (E) you cannot expect a high grade to be your achievement

5. Before traveling to Germany for Christmas, the church choir rehearsed constantly their German carols.

   (A) rehearsed constantly their German carols
   (B) constantly rehearsed their German carols
   (C) rehearsed German carols over and over again
   (D) held rehearsals constantly in German to learn their carols
   (E) were constantly holding rehearsals to learn their carols

6. The guests criticized the hotel manager for failing to replace the beds nor remove the old mattresses.

   (A) nor remove
   (B) nor removing
   (C) nor the removal of
   (D) or by removing
   (E) and to remove

7. Math and science are an example of fields that have a shortage of qualified teachers.

   (A) are an example of fields that
   (B) exemplify fields where we
   (C) are examples of fields that
   (D) exemplifies fields where we
   (E) are examples of fields where we

8. Last year, one of my students were sick so often that I were concerned he might not be promoted to the next grade.

   (A) were sick so often that I were concerned he might
   (B) was sick so often that I was concerned he might
   (C) were sick so often; that I was concerned he might
   (D) was sick so often, I was concerned he might
   (E) was sick so often; I were concerned he might

9. Professor Wesley placed a premium on brevity, insisting his students edit their essays thoroughly for eliminating all non-essential words.

   (A) for eliminating all non-essential words
   (B) to eliminate all non-essential words
   (C) having to eliminate all non-essential edits
   (D) in eliminating all non-essential words
   (E) to eliminate the non-essential use of words

10. As a journalist, Sidney is alarming to see how many high school students cannot write a coherent sentence.

   (A) Sidney is alarming to see how many
   (B) Sidney finds it alarming that there are so many
   (C) Sidney was alarmed by how many
   (D) it alarms Sidney that many
   (E) Sidney was alarmed to see how many

Check the Answer Key on the next page.

ANSWER KEY
Shortcut #6: Speed Practice Drill C

	Best Choices	Answer
1.	A or E	A
2.	A or B	A
3.	A or C	C
4.	A or D	D
5.	A or B	B
6.	A or E	E
7.	A or C	A
8.	A or B	B
9.	A or B	B – *use "ing" to rule out A*
10.	A or E	E – *use "ing" to rule out A*

SCORE BOX

Correct Answers	Raw Points	Scaled Points
1	1	10
2	2	20
3	3	30
4	4	40
5	5	50
6	6	60
7	7	70
8	8	80
9	9	90
10	10	100

_____ Your Total   _____ Your Raw Points   _____ Points Added to Your SAT Score!

Practice in Your SAT Workbooks

After completing the 3 practice drills, you are the ***all-seeing, all-knowing,*** newly-minted **MASTER** of Shortcut #6. Now you can put it to work for you.

Go to any SAT workbook and scan the reading sections to see more examples of Shortcut #6. The more examples you see, the more this Shortcut will ***stick*** in your mind and pop out at you in the answer choices.

Nike tells you: ***Just do it!***

Dr. Jay tells you: ***Just use it!***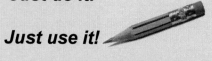

Just use it on every practice test you take, and you will be ready to snap up Shortcut #6 hidden inside your SAT test.

No Shortcut is Foolproof

Just as there are exceptions to every rule, you could
possibly find an exception to **Shortcut #6.**

MATH SHORTCUT #7

SECRET PATTERN:

5 CONSECUTIVE NUMBERS in the ANSWER CHOICES:

(A) 3

(B) 4

(C) 5

(D) 6

(E) 7

SECRET TWIST: This rule also applies when *only the first digit in the numbers are consecutive*. For example: (A) 1.5, (B) 2.5, (C) 3.5, (D) 4.5, (E) 5.5. In this example, the correct answer is *still* (B), (C), or (D).

Before you start to use the process of elimination (POE) to answer an SAT math question or decide to skip a question, take *2 seconds* to scan the answer choices for this **secret pattern**: *ALL 5 answer choices are consecutive numbers.*

DETECT

answers (A), (B), (C), (D), (E) are all consecutive numbers.

PREDICT

(B), (C), or (D) is the correct answer.

Rule out the other answer choices!

DECIDE

either (B), (C), or (D).

If you are clueless, just pick (B), (C), or (D). You **have a 33% chance** to select the correct answer – without thinking about the choices!

If you have a clue to tip your decision in favor of (B), (C) or (D), you have a **much higher than 33% chance** to select the correct answer.

SCORE

1 correct answer	*gives you*	1 (raw) point
1 (raw) point	*roughly adds*	10 points to your SAT score!

The following 3 examples of Shortcut #7 are SNAPSHOTS that show you how extremely easy it is to recognize the **secret pattern** Shortcut #7 is based on: **ALL 5 answer choices are consecutive numbers**.

Example #1: BEFORE

Before you recognize the Shortcut, the SAT question is **difficult**. It is longer and harder to answer with 5 possible answers to read and think about.

1. If……………, what is the value of x?

   (A) 5
   (B) 6
   (C) 7
   (D) 8
   (E) 9

After you recognize the Shortcut, the question is **simple**. It is shorter and easier to answer with only 3 possible answers to read and think about.

   1. If……………., what is the value of x?
      (B) 6
      (C) 7
      (D) 8

In 2 seconds, Shortcut #7 turns HARD questions you SKIPPED on your last SAT test into EASY questions you can answer on your next SAT test!

Before you start to use the process of elimination (POE) to answer an SAT math question or decide to skip a question, take *2 seconds* to scan the answer choices for this **secret pattern**: *ALL 5 answer choices are consecutive numbers.*

DETECT

answers (A), (B), (C), (D), (E) are all consecutive numbers.

PREDICT

(B), (C), or (D) is the correct answer.
Rule out the other answer choices!

DECIDE

either (B), (C), or (D).

When you are totally clueless, just pick (B), (C), or (D).
By the law of chance, you still **get a 33% chance** to select the correct answer.

When you have a clue to tip your decision in favor of (B), (C), or (D), go for it.
By using a bit of knowledge, you get a **much higher than 33% chance** to select the correct answer.

SCORE

| 1 correct answer | *gives you* | 1(raw) point |
| 1 (raw) point | *roughly adds* | 10 points to your SAT score! |

Example #2: BEFORE

Before you recognize the Shortcut, the SAT question is **difficult**. It is longer and harder to answer with 5 possible answers to read and think about.

2. If…………., what is the value of y?

    (A) 1.3
    (B) 2.3
    (C) 3.3
    (D) 4.3
    (E) 5.3

Example #2: AFTER

After you recognize the Shortcut, the question is **simple**. It is shorter and easier to answer with only 3 possible answers to read and think about.

2. If…………., what is the value of y?

    (B) 2.3
    (C) 3.3
    (D) 4.3

Before you start to use the process of elimination (POE) to answer an SAT math question or decide to skip a question, take *2 seconds* to scan the answer choices for this **secret pattern**: *ALL 5 answer choices are consecutive numbers.*

DETECT

the **SECRET TWIST: all 5 answer choices are not TRUE consecutive numbers, but the first digits of each answer are consecutive.**

PREDICT

(B), (C), or (D) is the correct answer.
Rule out the other answer choices!

DECIDE

either (B), (C), or (D).

When you are totally clueless, just pick (B), (C), or (D).
By the law of chance, you get a **33% chance** to select the correct answer.

When you have a clue to tip your decision in favor of (B), (C), or (D), go for it.
By using a bit of knowledge, you get a **much higher than 33% chance** to select the correct answer.

SCORE

| 1 correct answer | *gives you* | 1(raw) point |
| 1 (raw) point | *roughly adds* | 10 points to your SAT score! |

Example #3: BEFORE

Before you recognize the Shortcut, the SAT question is **difficult**. It is longer and harder to answer with 5 possible answers to read and think about.

    3. If...........,, what is the value of $x + y - 2$?

        (A) 3
        (B) 4
        (C) 5
        (D) 6
        (E) 7

Example #3: AFTER

After you recognize the Shortcut, the question is **simple**. It is shorter and easier to answer with only 3 possible answers to read and think about.

    3. If..........., what is the value of $x + y - 2$?

        (B) 4
        (C) 5
        (D) 6

Before you start to use the process of elimination (POE) to answer an SAT math question or decide to skip a question, take *2 seconds* to scan the answer choices for this **secret pattern**: *ALL 5 answer choices are consecutive numbers.*

DETECT

answers (A), (B), (C), (D), (E) are all consecutive numbers.

PREDICT

(B), (C), or (D) is the correct answer.
Rule out the other answer choices!

DECIDE

either (B), (C), or (D).

When you are totally clueless, just pick (B), (C), or (D).
By the law of chance, you still **get a 33% chance** to select the correct answer.

When you have a clue to tip your decision in favor of (B), (C), or (D), go for it.
By using a bit of knowledge, you get a **much higher than 33% chance** to select the correct answer.

SCORE

| 1 correct answer | *gives you* | 1(raw) point |
| 1 (raw) point | *roughly adds* | 10 points to your SAT score! |

The POWER of KNOWING How to Analyze Answer Choices

After seeing Shortcut #7, you have the power of knowing exactly which **secret pattern** to look for in the answer choices that will give you an instant opportunity to score you never recognized before in SAT questions.

Shortcut #7: Speed Practice Drills

Now it is time to practice using Shortcut #7 to access opportunities to score on your SAT in *2 seconds – as fast as you click on Google or tap an app on your smartphone*. The questions in the drills are designed to develop your ability to rapidly scan the answer choices to detect this Shortcut to the correct answer: *all 5 answer choices are consecutive numbers*.

The repetition built into the 3 drills will make scanning the answer choices for Shortcut #7 a part of your test-taking routine – a new habit to SCORE FAST. The faster you can snap up Shortcut #7 in the following drills, the better prepared you will be to take advantage of this Shortcut on your SAT test.

Math Shortcut #7:
Speed Practice Drill A

Directions:

▶▶ Set your timer or timer app for 60 seconds.

▶▶ Underline answer choices (B), (C), and (D) in each question.

▶▶ Circle 1 answer choice – without thinking about the choices.

Experience the awesome chance you get to score a point the second you spot this Shortcut in the following questions.

---

1. When a certain number is increased by…………, what is the number?

   (A) 12
   (B) 13
   (C) 14
   (D) 15
   (E) 16

2. In the figure above ……….. ,what is the value of x?

   (A) −5
   (B) −6
   (C) −7
   (D) −8
   (E) −9

3. In the figure above ……….., what is the value of b/a?

   (A) $^1/5$
   (B) $^2/5$
   (C) $^3/5$
   (D) $^4/5$
   (E) $^5/5$

4. If……..…….., then what is the value of $x + y$?

   (A) 7
   (B) 8
   (C) 9
   (D) 10
   (E) 11

5. If $x =$ … and $y =$ …., what is the value of ……….. z ?

   (A) 10
   (B) 11
   (C) 12
   (D) 13
   (E) 14

6. What is the y-intercept if …………?

   (A) 21
   (B) 22
   (C) 23
   (D) 24
   (E) 25

---

7. If x is …..……, what is the value of y?

    (A) 13
    (B) 14
    (C) 15
    (D) 16
    (E) 17

8. If ………., then $x + y =$

    (A) 8
    (B) 9
    (C) 10
    (D) 11
    (E) 12

9. If………., which of the following is the greatest?

    (A) $1 + x$
    (B) $2 + x$
    (C) $3 + x$
    (D) $4 + x$
    (E) $5 + x$

10. If $p = …$ and $n = …$, what is the value of m?

    (A) 5
    (B) 6
    (C) 7
    (D) 8
    (E) 9

Check the Answer Key on the next page.

ANSWER KEY
Math Shortcut #7: Speed Practice Drill A

Best Choices	Answer
1. B, C, or D	B
2. B, C, or D	C
3. B, C, or D	D – Secret Twist!
4. B, C, or D	D
5. B, C, or D	C
6. B, C, or D	B
7. B, C, or D	C
8. B, C, or D	D
9. B, C, or D	B
10. B, C, or D	C

SCORE BOX

Correct Answers	Raw Points	Scaled Points
1	1	10
2	2	20
3	3	30
4	4	40
5	5	50
6	6	60
7	7	70
8	8	80
9	9	90
10	10	100

_____Your Total   ____Your Raw Points   _____ Points Added to Your SAT Score!

Math Shortcut #7:
Speed Practice Drill B

1. If ………….., at what value does m cross the x-axis?

   (A) 1
   (B) 2
   (C) 3
   (D) 4
   (E) 5

2. If ………….., which of the following is a possible value of $x^2 - x$?

   (A) 30
   (B) 40
   (C) 50
   (D) 60
   (E) 70

3. What is the y-intercept when……..?

   (A) 4
   (B) 5
   (C) 6
   (D) 7
   (E) 8

4. Which of the following satisfies the relationship between A and B above?

   (A) D = c + 1
   (B) D = c + 2
   (C) D = c + 3
   (D) D = c + 4
   (E) D = c + 5

5. If $a + b = -1$, then ……

   (A) 1.5
   (B) 2.5
   (C) 3.5
   (D) 4.5
   (E) 5.5

6. If …….....…, what is the value of x?

   (A) 300
   (B) 400
   (C) 500
   (D) 600
   (E) 700

7. If ...., what is the value of t?

   (A) 1
   (B) 2
   (C) 3
   (D) 4
   (E) 5

8. Let the function be defined by.........,
   what is the value of x?

   (A) 22
   (B) 23
   (C) 24
   (D) 25
   (E) 26

9. If .... , and............,what is the value
   of x?

   (A) 31
   (B) 32
   (C) 33
   (D) 34
   (E) 35

10. If m is greater than 2, then.......

   (A) $m + 3$
   (B) $m + 4$
   (C) $m + 5$
   (D) $m + 6$
   (E) $m + 7$

Check the Answer Key on the next page.

ANSWER KEY
Math Shortcut #7: Speed Practice Drill B

	Best Choices	Answer
1.	B, C, or D	D
2.	B, C, or D	C – Secret Twist!
3.	B, C, or D	A
4.	B, C, or D	D
5.	B, C, or D	A – Secret Twist!
6.	B, C, or D	C – Secret Twist!
7.	B, C, or D	B
8.	B, C, or D	B
9.	B, C, or D	D
10.	B, C, or D	C

SCORE BOX

Correct Answers	Raw Points	Scaled Points
1	1	10
2	2	20
3	3	30
4	4	40
5	5	50
6	6	60
7	7	70
8	8	80
9	9	90
10	10	100

_____Your Total   _____Your Raw Points   _____ Points Added to Your SAT Score!

Math Shortcut #7:
Speed Practice Drill C

1. If x and y can be defined by......., then......

   (A) 5
   (B) 6
   (C) 7
   (D) 8
   (E) 9

2. If the function of x is......., then......

   (A) 14
   (B) 15
   (C) 16
   (D) 17
   (E) 18

3. If x is.........., then what is the value of y?

   (A) 1.5
   (B) 2.5
   (C) 3.5
   (D) 4.5
   (E) 5.5

4. If........., which of the following is the values of p?

   (A) 1.5
   (B) 2.5
   (C) 3.5
   (D) 4.5
   (E) 5.5

5. If.........., which of the following cannot be a value of b?

   (A) –3
   (B) –4
   (C) –5
   (D) –6
   (E) –7

6. On the number line above.........., what is the value of m?

   (A) 0
   (B) 1
   (C) 2
   (D) 3
   (E) 4

7. If………., which of the numbers has the least value?

    (A) $1z$

    (B) $2z$

    (C) $3z$

    (D) $4z$

    (E) $5z$

8. In the set of numbers above…….., what is the value of x?

    (A) 22

    (B) 23

    (C) 24

    (D) 25

    (E) 26

9. When a number is increased by………., what is the number?

    (A) −1

    (B) −2

    (C) −3

    (D) −4

    (E) −5

10. If $m = $…………, what is the result when………?

    (A) $m + 1$

    (B) $m + 2$

    (C) $m + 3$

    (D) $m + 4$

    (E) $m + 5$

Check the Answer Key on the next page.

ANSWER KEY
Math Shortcut #7: Speed Practice Drill C

Best Choices	Answer
1. B, C, or D	B
2. B, C, or D	C
3. B, C, or D	D – Secret Twist!
4. B, C, or D	C – Secret Twist!
5. B, C, or D	B
6. B, C, or D	B
7. B, C, or D	D
8. B, C, or D	C
9. B, C, or D	D
10. B, C, or D	C

SCORE BOX

Correct Answers	Raw Points	Scaled Points
1	1	10
2	2	20
3	3	30
4	4	40
5	5	50
6	6	60
7	7	70
8	8	80
9	9	90
10	10	100

_____ Your Total   _____ Your Raw Points   _____ Points Added to
Your SAT Score!

Practice in Your SAT Workbooks

After completing the 3 practice drills, you are the *all-seeing, all-knowing,* newly-minted **MASTER** of Shortcut #7. Now you can put it to work for you.

Go to any SAT workbook and scan the reading sections to see more examples of Shortcut #7. The more examples you see, the more this Shortcut will *stick* in your mind and pop out at you in the answer choices.

Nike tells you: *Just do it!*

Dr. Jay tells you: *Just use it!*

Just use it on every practice test you take, and you will be ready to snap up Shortcut #7 hidden inside your SAT test.

No Shortcut is Foolproof

Just as there are exceptions to every rule, you could possibly find an exception to **Shortcut #7.**

MATH SHORTCUT #8

SECRET PATTERN:

ONLY the FIRST 3 ANSWER CHOICES are CONSECUTIVE NUMBERS:

(A)   1

(B)   2

(C)   3

(D) xx

(E) xx

NOTE: This Shortcut is similar to Shortcut #7, but in Shortcut #8 ALL 5 of the answer choices are in consecutive order. In this Shortcut, ONLY the FIRST 3 answer choices are in consecutive order.

Before you start to use the process of elimination (POE) to answer an SAT math question or decide to skip a question, take *2 seconds* to scan the answer choices for this **secret pattern**:

ONLY the FIRST 3 answer choices are consecutive numbers.

DETECT

(A), (B), and (C) are consecutive numbers.

PREDICT

(A), (B), or (C) is the correct answer.

Rule out the other answer choices!

DECIDE

either (A), (B), or (C).

If you are clueless, just pick (A), (B), or (C). You **have a 33% chance** to select the correct answer – without thinking about the choices!

If you have a clue to tip your decision in favor of (A), (B), or (C), you have a **much higher than 33% chance** to select the correct answer.

SCORE

| 1 correct answer | *gives you* | 1 (raw) point |
| 1 (raw) point | *roughly adds* | 10 points to your SAT score! |

The following 3 examples of Shortcut #8 are SNAPSHOTS that show you how extremely easy it is to recognize the **secret pattern** Shortcut #8 is based on: **only the first 3 answer choices are consecutive numbers.**

Example #1: BEFORE

Before you recognize the Shortcut, the SAT question is **difficult**. It is longer and harder to answer with 5 possible answers to read and think about.

1. If x and y are positive integers…., which of the following could be the value of x?

   (A) 2
   (B) 3
   (C) 4
   (D) 7
   (E) 8

Example #1: AFTER

Example #1: After you recognize the Shortcut, the question is **simple**. It is shorter and easier to answer with only 2 possible answers to read and think about.

1. If x and y are positive integers.........,which of the following could be the value of x?

    (A) **2**
    (B) **3**
    (C) **4**

In 2 seconds, Shortcut #8 turns HARD questions you SKIPPED on your <u>last SAT</u> test into EASY questions <u>you can answer</u> on your <u>next SAT test</u>!

Before you start to use the process of elimination (POE) to answer an SAT math question or decide to skip a question, take *2 seconds* to scan the answer choices for this **secret pattern**: *ONLY the first 3 answer choices are consecutive numbers.*

DETECT

(A), (B), and (C) are consecutive numbers.

PREDICT

(A), (B), or (C) is the correct answer.

Rule out the other answer choices!

DECIDE

either (A), (B), or (C).

When you are totally clueless, just pick (A), (B), or (C).
By the law of chance, you still **get a 33% chance** to select the correct answer.

When you have a clue to tip your decision in favor of (A), (B), or (C), go for it.
By using a bit of knowledge, you get a **much higher than 33% chance** to select the correct answer.

SCORE

| 1 correct answer | *gives you* | 1(raw) point |
| 1 (raw) point | *roughly adds* | 10 points to your SAT score! |

Before you recognize the Shortcut, the SAT question is **difficult**. It is longer and harder to answer with 5 possible answers to read and think about.

2. If p is a positive number divisible by 4, ..., what is the greatest possible value of p?

    (A) 45
    (B) 46
    (C) 47
    (D) 52
    (E) 60

After you recognize the Shortcut, the question is **simple**. It is shorter and easier to answer with only 2 possible answers to read and think about.

2. If p is a positive number divisible by 4, ..., what is the greatest possible value of p?

    (A) 45
    (B) 46
    (C) 47

Before you start to use the process of elimination (POE) to answer a question or decide to skip a question, take *2 seconds* to scan the answer choices for this **secret pattern:** *ONLY the first 3 answer choices are consecutive numbers.*

DETECT

(A), (B), and (C) are consecutive numbers.

PREDICT

(A), (B), or (C) is the correct answer.
Rule out the other answer choices!

DECIDE

either (A), (B), or (C).

When you are totally clueless, just pick (A), (B), or (C).
By the law of chance, you still **get a 33% chance** to select the correct answer.

When you have a clue to tip your decision in favor of (A), (B), or (C), go for it.
By using a bit of knowledge, you get a **much higher than 33% chance** to select the correct answer.

SCORE

| 1 correct answer | *gives you* | 1(raw) point |
| 1 (raw) point | *roughly adds* | 10 points to your SAT score! |

Example #3: BEFORE

Before you recognize the Shortcut, the SAT question is **difficult**. It is longer and harder to answer with 5 possible answers to read and think about.

3. If set *J* consists of.........., how many integers are in set *J*?

    (A)   0
    (B)   1
    (C)   2
    (D)   4
    (E) −6

Example #3: AFTER

After you recognize the Shortcut, the question is **simple**. It is shorter and easier to answer with only 2 possible answers to read and think about.

3. If set *J* consists of.........., how many integers are in set *J*?

    (A) 0
    (B) 1
    (C) 2

Before you start to use the process of elimination (POE) to answer an SAT math question or decide to skip a question, take *2 seconds* to scan the answer choices for this **secret pattern**: *ONLY the first 3 answer choices are consecutive numbers.*

DETECT

(A), (B), and (C) are consecutive numbers.

PREDICT

(A), (B), or (C) is the correct answer.
Rule out the other answer choices!

DECIDE

either (A), (B), or (C).

When you are totally clueless, just pick (A), (B), or (C).
By the law of chance, you still **get a 33% chance** to select the correct answer.

When you have a clue to tip your decision in favor of (A), (B), or (C), go for it.
By using a bit of knowledge, you get a **much higher than 33% chance** to select the correct answer.

SCORE

| 1 correct answer | *gives you* | 1(raw) point |
| 1 (raw) point | *roughly adds* | 10 points to your SAT score! |

The POWER of KNOWING How to Analyze Answer Choices

After seeing Shortcut #8, you have the power of knowing exactly which **secret pattern** to look for in the answer choices that will give you an instant opportunity to score you never recognized before in SAT questions.

Shortcut #8: Speed Practice Drills

Now it is time to practice using Shortcut #8 to access opportunities to score on your SAT in *2 seconds – as fast as you click on Google or tap an app* on *your smartphone.* The questions in the following drills are designed to develop your ability to rapidly scan the answer choices to detect this Shortcut to the correct answers: *only the first 3 answer choices are consecutive numbers.*

The repetition built into the 3 drills will make scanning the answer choices for Shortcut #8 a part of your test-taking routine – a new habit to SCORE FAST. The faster you can snap up Shortcut #8 in the following drills, the better prepared you will be to take advantage of this Shortcut on your SAT test.

Directions:

⏩   Set your timer or timer app for 60 seconds.

⏩   Underline answer choices (A), (B), and (C) in each question.

⏩   Circle 1 answer choice — without thinking about the choices.

Experience the awesome chance you get to score a point the second you spot this Shortcut in the following questions.

1. In the figure above ...., what is the value of x?

    (A)   2
    (B)   3
    (C)   4
    (D)   8
    (E)   10
    (F)   12

2. For the numbers listed above,......., what is the value of n?

    (A)   6
    (B)   7
    (C)   8
    (D)   16
    (E)   18

3. For the positive integers,.......which of the following is equal to $x-y$?

    (A)   1+1
    (B)   2+2
    (C)   3+3
    (D)   6+6
    (E)   9+9

4. In the circle above..........., what is the ratio?

    (A)   1 to 4
    (B)   1 to 5
    (C)   1 to 6
    (D)   1 to 9
    (E)   1 to 10

5. If x and y are ....,, what is the value of x?

    (A)   1
    (B)   2
    (C)   3
    (D)   5
    (E)   7

6. In the diagram above, ...what is the value of the 3 pairs?

    (A)   16
    (B)   17
    (C)   18
    (D)   24
    (E)   25

7. In the equation above,.......... what is the value of *z?*

   (A) 8
   (B) 9
   (C) 10
   (D) 22
   (E) 33

8. In the polygon above............, how many triangles are formed?

   (A) four
   (B) five
   (C) six
   (D) eighteen
   (E) twenty

9. In the operation described above,.........., what is the value of *x?*

   (A) 0
   (B) 1
   (C) 2
   (D) 4
   (E) 6

10. When an integer is............, what number results?

   (A) 1
   (B) 2
   (C) 3
   (D) 7
   (E) 13

Check the Answer Key on the next page.

Best Choices	Answer
1. A, B, or C	B
2. A, B, or C	C
3. A, B, or C	A
4. A, B, or C	B
5. A, B, or C	C
6. A, B, or C	A
7. A, B, or C	B
8. A, B, or C	C
9. A, B, or C	A
10. A, B, or C	C

SCORE BOX

Correct Answers	Raw Points	Scaled Points
1	1	10
2	2	20
3	3	30
4	4	40
5	5	50
6	6	60
7	7	70
8	8	80
9	9	90
10	10	100

_____ Your Total   _____ Your Raw Points   _____ Points Added to Your SAT Score!

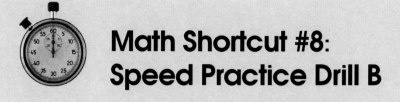
Directions:

▶▶ Set your timer or timer app for 40 seconds.

▶▶ Underline answer choices (A), (B), and (C) in each question.

▶▶ Circle 1 answer choice — without thinking about the choices.

Experience the awesome chance you get to score a point the second you spot this Shortcut in the following questions.

1. If a and b are……….., what is the value of *a?*

    (A) 3
    (B) 4
    (C) 5
    (D) 10
    (E) 15

2. What is the value of *m,* if …………… ?

    (A) 14
    (B) 15
    (C) 16
    (D) 20
    (E) 24

3. If *s* is a positive number, then *v* =

    (A) 1
    (B) 2
    (C) 3
    (D) 11
    (E) 11.5

4. If ……………, which of the following is a possible value of *x?*

    (A) 4
    (B) 5
    (C) 6
    (D) 8
    (E) 10

5. If ……….., which of the following is a possible value of *y?*

    (A) 6
    (B) 7
    (C) 8
    (D) 13
    (E) 14

6. If the points of intersection are………, what is the value of *K?*

    (A) 12
    (B) 13
    (C) 14
    (D) 22
    (E) 25

7. If a triangle ...., what is the length of 1 side of the triangle?

   (A) 2
   (B) 3
   (C) 4
   (D) 9.5
   (E) 11.5

8. In the figure above, what is the length of *CD*?

   (A) 0
   (B) 1
   (C) 2
   (D) 4
   (E) 5

9. In the graph above, what is the value of *Z*?

   (A) 4
   (B) 5
   (C) 6
   (D) 15
   (E) 23

10. If ...., which is the greatest number that can result?

   (A) 5
   (B) 6
   (C) 7
   (D) 9
   (E) 11

Check the Answer Key on the next page.

ANSWER KEY
Math Shortcut #8: Speed Practice Drill B

	Best Choices	Answer
1.	A, B, or C	B
2.	A, B, or C	A
3.	A, B, or C	C
4.	A, B, or C	A
5.	A, B, or C	B
6.	A, B, or C	C
7.	A, B, or C	C
8.	A, B, or C	A
9.	A, B, or C	B
10.	A, B, or C	B

SCORE BOX

Correct Answers	Raw Points	Scaled Points
1	1	10
2	2	20
3	3	30
4	4	40
5	5	50
6	6	60
7	7	70
8	8	80
9	9	90
10	10	100

_____ Your Total   _____ Your Raw Points   _____ Points Added to Your SAT Score!

Math Shortcut #8:
Speed Practice Drill C

1. If a linear function................, what is the value of $x - y$?

   (A) 1
   (B) 2
   (C) 3
   (D) 6. 5
   (E) 7. 7

2. In the figure above, what is the value of Z?

   (A) 6
   (B) 7
   (C) 8
   (D) 11
   (E) 12

3. If m is a positive integer, then...........
   could equal which of the following?

   (A) 12
   (B) 13
   (C) 14
   (D) 16
   (E) 19

4. In the above graph, what is the number of cases?

   (A) 0
   (B) 1
   (C) 2
   (D) 4
   (E) 6

5. In a standard plane, ...what is the length of AB?

   (A) 6
   (B) 7
   (C) 8
   (D) 41
   (E) 42

6. If a, b, and c are............., what is the value of c?

   (A) 3
   (B) 4
   (C) 5
   (D) 10
   (E) 15

7. If fruit was added, …………………,
   what is the weight of the basket?

   (A) six pounds
   (B) seven pounds
   (C) eight pounds
   (D) eleven pounds
   (E) thirteen pounds

8. For the triangle above, what is the length
   of AB?

   (A) 4
   (B) 5
   (C) 6
   (D) 9
   (E) 13

9. If 3 times………, what is the number?

   (A) 2
   (B) 3
   (C) 4
   (D) 13
   (E) 20

10. In the number line above,…………what
    is the value of $-x$?

    (A) 8
    (B) 9
    (C) 10
    (D) 12
    (E) 14

Check the Answer Key on the next page.

Best Choices	Answer
1. A, B, or C	B
2. A, B, or C	B
3. A, B, or C	C
4. A, B, or C	A
5. A, B, or C	C
6. A, B, or C	A
7. A, B, or C	C
8. A, B, or C	A
9. A, B, or C	B
10. A, B, or C	C

SCORE BOX

Correct Answers	Raw Points	Scaled Points
1	1	10
2	2	20
3	3	30
4	4	40
5	5	50
6	6	60
7	7	70
8	8	80
9	9	90
10	10	100

_____ Your Total   _____ Your Raw Points   _____ Points Added to Your SAT Score!

Practice in Your SAT Workbooks

After completing the 3 practice drills, you are the ***all-seeing, all-knowing,*** newly-minted **MASTER** of Shortcut #8. Now you can put it to work for you.

Go to any SAT workbook and scan the reading sections to see more examples of Shortcut #8. The more examples you see, the more this Shortcut will ***stick*** in your mind and pop out at you in your practice tests.

Nike tells you: *Just do it!*

Dr. Jay tells you: *Just use it!*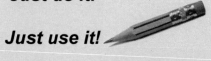

Just use it on every practice test you take, and you will be ready to snap up Shortcut #8 hidden inside your SAT test.

No Shortcut is Foolproof

Just as there are exceptions to every rule, you could possibly find an exception to **Shortcut #8.**

MATH SHORTCUT #9

SECRET PATTERN:

2 ANSWER CHOICES that are ALIKE Except for ONLY 1 DIFFERENCE:

(A) xxxxxxxxxxxxxx

(B) $x + b + (9 + \boxed{14})$

(C) $x + b + (9 + \boxed{3})$

(D) xxxxxxxxxxxxxx

(E) xxxxxxxxxxxxxx

Before you start to use the process of elimination (POE) to answer an SAT math question or decide to skip a question, take *2 seconds* to scan the answer choices for this **secret pattern**: *2 answer choices are ALIKE, except for only 1 difference between them.*

DETECT

2 answer choices (we'll call them X and Y) are ALIKE, except for only 1 difference between them.

PREDICT

X or Y is the correct answer.

Rule out the other answer choices!

DECIDE

either X or Y.

If you are clueless, just pick X or Y. You **have a 50% chance** to select the correct answer – without thinking about either choice!

If you have a clue to tip your decision in favor of X or Y, you have a **much higher than 50% chance** to select the correct answer.

SCORE

| 1 correct answer | *gives you* | 1 (raw) point |
| 1 (raw) point | *roughly adds* | 10 points to your SAT score! |

The following 3 examples of Shortcut #9 are SNAPSHOTS that show you how extremely easy it is to recognize the **secret pattern** Shortcut #9 is based on: **2 answer choices are ALIKE with only 1 difference between them.**

Example #1: BEFORE

Before you recognize the Shortcut, the SAT question is **difficult**. It is longer and harder to answer with 5 possible answers to read and think about.

1. The figure above is a rectangle, what is the value of *x*?

   (A) √5

   (B) 8/3

   (C) 7

   (D) 2√5

   (E) 5

Example #1: AFTER

After you recognize the Shortcut, the question is **simple**. It is shorter and easier to answer with only 2 possible answers to read and think about.

1. Which of the following is equal to *3x + 9y +12*?

    (A) $\sqrt{5}$

    (D) $2\sqrt{5}$

In 2 seconds, Shortcut #9 turns HARD questions you SKIPPED on your <u>last SAT</u> test into EASY questions <u>you can answer</u> on your <u>next SAT test!</u>

Before you start to use the process of elimination (POE) to answer an SAT math question or decide to skip a question, take *2 seconds* to scan the answer choices for this **secret pattern**: *2 answer choices are ALIKE, except for only 1 difference between them.*

DETECT

"$\sqrt{5}$" in (A) and (D).

PREDICT

(A) or (D) is the correct answer.
Rule out the other answer choices!

DECIDE

either (A) or (D).

When you are totally clueless, just pick (A) or (D).
By the law of chance, you get a **great 50% chance** to select the correct answer.

When you have a clue to tip your decision in favor of (A) or (D), go for it.
By using a bit of knowledge, you get a **much higher than 50% chance** to select the correct answer.

SCORE

| 1 correct answer | *gives you* | 1(raw) point |
| 1 (raw) point | *roughly adds* | 10 points to your SAT score! |

Example #2: BEFORE

Before you recognize the Shortcut, the SAT question is **difficult**. It is longer and harder to answer with 5 possible answers to read and think about.

2. In the figure above, ...,what is the area of the black portion of the circle?

(A) 3
(B)   π/4
(C) 2
(D) 3 π/4
(E) 4 π

Example #2: AFTER

After you recognize the Shortcut, the question is **simple**. It is shorter and easier to answer with only 2 possible answers to read and think about.

2. In the figure above,........., what is the area of the black portion of the circle?

(B)   π/4
(D) 3 π/4

Before you start to use the process of elimination (POE) to answer an SAT math question or decide to skip a question, take *2 seconds* to scan the answer choices for this **secret pattern**: *2 answer choices are ALIKE, except for only one difference between them.*

DETECT

"π /4" in (B) and (D).

PREDICT

(B) or (D) is the correct answer.
Rule out the other answer choices!

DECIDE

either (B) or (D).

When you are totally clueless, just pick (B) or (D).

By the law of chance, you get a **great 50% chance** to select the correct answer.

When you have a clue to tip your decision in favor of (B) or (D), go for it.

By using a bit of knowledge, you get a **much higher than 50% chance** to select the correct answer.

SCORE

| 1 correct answer | *gives you* | 1(raw) point |
| 1 (raw) point | *roughly adds* | 10 points to your SAT score! |

Example #2: BEFORE

Before you recognize the Shortcut, the SAT question is **difficult**. It is longer and harder to answer with 5 possible answers to read and think about.

1. If.........., what is 20 percent of x?

    (A) $1.2x$
    (B) $20x$
    (C) $12x$
    (D) $12.5x$
    (E) $15x$

Example #2: AFTER

After you recognize the Shortcut, the question is **simple**. It is shorter and easier to answer with only 2 possible answers to read and think about.

3. If ...., what is 20 percent of x?

    (C) $12x$
    (D) $12.5x$

Before you start to use the process of elimination (POE) to answer an SAT math question or decide to skip a question, take *2 seconds* to scan the answer choices for this **secret pattern**: *2 answer choices are ALIKE, except for only 1 difference between them.*

DETECT

"12x" in (C) and (D).

PREDICT

(C) or (D) is the correct answer.
Rule out the other answer choices!

DECIDE

either (C) or (D).

When you are totally clueless, just pick (C) or (D).
By the law of chance, you get a **great 50% chance** to select the correct answer.

When you have a clue to tip your decision in favor of (C) or (D), go for it.
By using a bit of knowledge, you get a **much higher than 50% chance** to select the correct answer.

SCORE

1 correct answer	*gives you*	1(raw) point
1 (raw) point	*roughly adds*	10 points to your SAT score!

The POWER of KNOWING How to Analyze Answer Choices

After seeing Shortcut #9, you have the power of knowing exactly which **secret pattern** to look for in the answer choices that will give you an instant opportunity to score you never recognized before in SAT questions.

Shortcut #9: Speed Practice Drills

Now it is time to practice using Shortcut #9 to access opportunities to score on your SAT in *2 seconds – as fast as you click on Google or tap an app on your smartphone.* The questions in the drills are designed to develop your ability to rapidly scan the answer choices and detect this Shortcut to the answer: *2 almost identical answer choices with only 1 difference between them.*

The repetition built into the 3 drills will make scanning the answer choices for Shortcut #9 a part of your test-taking routine – a new habit to SCORE FAST. The faster you can snap up Shortcut #9 in the following drills, the better prepared you will be to take advantage of this Shortcut on your SAT test.

Math Shortcut #9:
Speed Practice Drill A

1. If ...., how many miles are the boys from the park?

   (A) 40
   (B) 51.5
   (C) 56.5
   (D) 75
   (E) 83

2. In the figure above............, what is the distance from vertex F to vertex G?

   (A) $3\sqrt{2}$
   (B) $3\sqrt{3}$
   (C) 4
   (D) 6
   (E) 7

3. In the figure above, what is the value of y .... ?

   (A) 108
   (B) 114
   (C) 117
   (D) 120
   (E) 135

4. If.............., what fraction of guests attended the dinner?

   (A) $^{13}/_{42}$
   (B) $^{1}/_{3}$
   (C) $^{5}/_{16}$
   (D) $^{8}/_{20}$
   (E) $^{17}/_{42}$

5. If............, which of the following represent the total charge?

   (A) $170z$
   (B) $160 + 20c$
   (C) $160 + 10$
   (D) $160 + 10z$
   (E) $170 + 30c$

6. In the figure above.........., what is the perimeter of $ABCD$?

   (A) 2
   (B) 4
   (C) 6
   (D) $8\sqrt{2}$
   (E) $10\sqrt{2}$

7. In the figure above…………, what is the perimeter of *CDEF*?

   (A) 6 *m*
   (B) 8 *m*
   (C) 12*m*
   (D) 15*m*
   (E) 20*m*

8. If …………, how many cups of flour were required in the recipe?

   (A) 6 $\frac{1}{2}$
   (B) 8
   (C) 10 $\frac{1}{3}$
   (D) 10 $\frac{2}{3}$
   (E) 12

9. If ……………, how many minutes will it take to fill the tank?

   (A) 4.3
   (B) 2.5
   (C) 1
   (D) 3.4
   (E) 4.7

10. If ….…………, what is the weight of the package in pounds?

    (A) 2 $\frac{1}{4}$
    (B) 4
    (C) 1 $\frac{1}{3}$
    (D) 6
    (E) 6 $\frac{3}{4}$

Check the Answer Key on page TK.

Best Choices	Answer
1. B or C	B
2. A or B	B
3. B or C	C
4. A or E	A
5. C or D	D
6. D or E	E
7. C or D	C
8. C or D	D
9. A or E	A
10. A or E	E

SCORE BOX

Correct Answers	Raw Points	Scaled Points
1	1	10
2	2	20
3	3	30
4	4	40
5	5	50
6	6	60
7	7	70
8	8	80
9	9	90
10	10	100

_____Your Total   _____Your Raw Points   _____ Points Added to Your SAT Score!

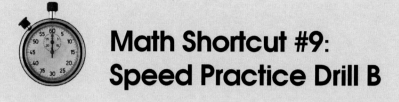

Math Shortcut #9: Speed Practice Drill B

Directions:

- Set your timer or timer app for 40 seconds.
- Underline the 2 answer choices that are alike except for 1 difference between them.
- Circle 1 answer choice — without thinking about either choice.

Experience the awesome 50/50 chance you get to score a point the second you spot this Shortcut in the following questions.

1. If ...., what is the length of the cord?

(A) 10 feet
(B) 15 feet
(C) 20 $\sqrt{2}$ feet
(D) 20 $\sqrt{3}$ feet
(E) 30 feet

2. If ...., what is the actual length that is represented?

(A) $2\frac{1}{2}$
(B) $4\frac{3}{5}$
(C) $6\frac{3}{4}$
(D) 8
(E) $10\frac{1}{2}$

3. In the figure above,.........What is the value of y/x?

(A) $\frac{4}{3}$
(B) $\frac{-4}{5}$
(C) 5
(D) $\frac{-7}{4}$
(E) 6

4. If x is increased by 20% and y is decreased by 20%, the resulting numbers will be equal. What is the ratio of x to y?

(A) $\frac{3}{4}$
(B) $\frac{3}{5}$
(C) $\frac{1}{1}$
(D) $\frac{4}{5}$
(E) $\frac{5}{3}$

5. If y = ..., then 2 y ....

(A) 36
(B) 48
(C) 130
(D) 134
(E) 200

6. A square cube has ...., what is the length of a diagonal AB?

(A) 4
(B) 5 $\sqrt{2}$
(C) 5 $\sqrt{3}$
(D) 6
(E) 11

7. If ...., what is the average of p, r, and s?

   (A) $p + r$

   (B) $p + x/5$

   (C) $p + 2x/5$

   (D) $p + 2r/2$

   (E) $2(p + x)$

8. In the rectangle above, what is the value of y?

   (A) $\sqrt{7}$

   (B) $4/5$

   (C) $\sqrt{3}$

   (D) $2/5$

   (E) $3/\sqrt{5}$

9. In the diagram above, what is the probability ....?

   (A) $5/10$

   (B) $8/10$

   (C) $9/12$

   (D) $11/15$

   (E) $16/20$

10. If ...., what is the value of $5x + 3y$?

   (A) 24

   (B) -5

   (C) $5/8$

   (D) -6

   (E) $7/8$

Check the Answer Key on the next page.

ANSWER KEY
Math Shortcut #9: Speed Practice Drill B

Best Choices	Answer
1. C or D	C
2. A or E	E
3. A or B	A
4. B or D	D
5. C or D	D
6. B or C	B
7. B or C	B
8. B or D	D
9. A or B	A
10. C or E	E

SCORE BOX

Correct Answers	Raw Points	Scaled Points
1	1	10
2	2	20
3	3	30
4	4	40
5	5	50
6	6	60
7	7	70
8	8	80
9	9	90
10	10	100

_____ Your Total   _____ Your Raw Points   _____ Points Added to Your SAT Score!

Math Shortcut #9:
Speed Practice Drill C

Directions:

⊳⊳ Set your timer or timer app for 30 seconds.

⊳⊳ Underline the 2 answer choices that are alike, except for 1 difference between them.

⊳⊳ Circle 1 answer choice — without thinking about either choice.

Experience the awesome 50/50 chance you get to score a point the second you spot this Shortcut in the following questions.

1. In the sequence………., how much greater is term *x* than term *z*?

   (A) 152
   (B) 167
   (C) 182
   (D) 330
   (E) 235

2. In the equation above, *m* is…………, what is the value of *x*?

   (A) 2
   (B) 5
   (C) 8
   (D) 13
   (E) 14

3. If $y + 2 =$ …………., what is the value of *y*?

   (A) 0.75
   (B) 1.22
   (C) 2.00
   (D) 3.00
   (E) 3.45

4. If x time is spent ………, how many minutes are spent online each day?

   (A) 46
   (B) 60
   (C) 120
   (D) 242
   (E) 342

5. If *x*, *y*, and *z* are……………., what is the greatest value of *z*

   (A) 18
   (B) 20
   (C) 34
   (D) 45
   (E) 47

6. If integer *k* is…………, what is the value of *m*?

   (A) −4
   (B) −2
   (C) 0
   (D) 2
   (E) 3

7. In the figure above…………, what is the value of $a + b + c + d$?

    (A)   46

    (B) 138

    (C) 264

    (D) 268

    (E) 311

8. If set X consists of …………, what is the probability ………..?

    (A) $^{19}\!/_{40}$

    (B) $^{29}\!/_{100}$

    (C) $^{2}\!/_{5}$

    (D) $^{9}\!/_{50}$

    (E) $^{21}\!/_{50}$

9. In the equation above …….., what is the relationship between x and y?

    (A) $x = 1y - 2$

    (B) $x = 1\,(y - 10)$

    (C) $x = 10 - 2y$

    (D) $x = 1\,(10 - y)$

    (E) $x = 10 - y$

10. In the figure above ……………., what is BC?

    (A)   4

    (B) $7\sqrt{2}$

    (C)   9

    (D) $12\sqrt{2}$

    (E) 15

Check the Answer Key on the next page.

ANSWER KEY
Math Shortcut #9: Speed Practice Drill C

	Best Choices	Answer
1.	A or C	A
2.	D or E	E
3.	C or D	C
4.	D or E	D
5.	D or E	E
6.	B or D	D
7.	C or D	C
8.	D or E	E
9.	C or E	E
10.	B or D	B

SCORE BOX

Correct Answers	Raw Points	Scaled Points
1	1	10
2	2	20
3	3	30
4	4	40
5	5	50
6	6	60
7	7	70
8	8	80
9	9	90
10	10	100

_____ Your Total   _____ Your Raw Points   _____ Points Added to Your SAT Score!

Practice in Your SAT Workbooks

After completing the 3 practice drills, you are the ***all-seeing, all-knowing,*** newly-minted **MASTER** of Shortcut #9. Now you can put it to work for you.

Go to any SAT workbook and scan the reading sections to see more examples of Shortcut #9. The more examples you see, the more this Shortcut will ***stick*** in your mind and pop out at you in the answer choices.

Nike tells you: ***Just do it!***

Dr. Jay tells you: ***Just use it!***

Just use it on every practice test you take, and you will be ready to snap up Shortcut #9 hidden inside your SAT test.

No Shortcut is Foolproof

Just as there are exceptions to every rule, you could possibly find an exception to **Shortcut #9.**

Mixed Math Speed Practice Drill: Shortcuts #7, #8 and #9

Now that you have learned Shortcuts #7, #8 and #9, it is time for a mixed review for you to practice choosing answers for math questions. The Speed Practice Drill will help you develop flexibility in your ability to snap up these Shortcuts in 2 seconds. Remember to follow the steps you've learned when answering the questions.

Mixed Math Speed Practice Drill: Shortcut #7, 8, and 9

Directions:

» Set your timer or timer app for 2 minutes.

» Underline Shortcut #7 (*all 5 answers are consecutive numbers*), Shortcut #8 (*only the first 3 answers are consecutive numbers*), and Shortcut #9 (*2 answer choices are alike except for 1 difference*). Some Shortcuts will pop out at you in 2 seconds, others may take a few more seconds.

» Circle 1 answer without thinking about the choices.

Experience the awesome chance you get to score a point the second you spot Shortcuts in the following questions.

1. If a triangle's sides are ………….., what is the length of the third side?

   (A) 11
   (B) 12
   (C) 13
   (D) 20
   (E) 34

2. If x is greater than 0 and …….., which of the following numbers has the greatest value?

   (A) $2 - x$
   (B) $2/x$
   (C) $-2/x$
   (D) x
   (E) $x2$

3. If p is …………, which of the following is the smallest in value?

   (A) $3/a$
   (B) $a/3$
   (C) $a + \frac{1}{2}$
   (D) $3/a + 1$
   (E) $3/a - 1$

4. In the figure above, what is the value of W?

   (A) 15
   (B) 16
   (C) 17
   (D) 18
   (E) 19

5. In the equation above, what is the value of b?

   (A) -2.5
   (B) -3.5
   (C) -4.5
   (D) -5.5
   (E) -6.5

6. If each box ……………….., how many cases are needed?

   (A) 1
   (B) 2
   (C) 3
   (D) 4
   (E) 5

7. If x is 2 less than r and ………………,
what is the value of m?

   (A) 11
   (B) 12
   (C) 13
   (D) 16
   (E) 20

8. If 2 rectangles, …………., what is the
value of x?

   (A) 20
   (B) 21
   (C) 22
   (D) 23
   (E) 24

9. If x is a negative number and ………..,
which of the following must be true?

   (A) $x < -4$
   (B) $x > 3.5$
   (C) $x < 2$
   (D) $x > 2$
   (E) $x > -5$

10. If a car dealership has …………., what
is the total number of cars?

   (A) 28
   (B) 29
   (C) 30
   (D) 46
   (E) 54

11. In the sequence above, the first term
is 6, and ………….. What is the value
of m?

   (A) 1
   (B) 2
   (C) 3
   (D) 6
   (E) 9

12. The lowest number in a set of consecutive
number is –15, if …………., how many
numbers are in this set?

   (A) 15
   (B) 16
   (C) 27
   (D) 33
   (E) 44

13. If x is ………………, what is the value
of x when $m = 4$.

   (A) –1
   (B) 0
   (C) 1
   (D) 4
   (E) 5

14. In the price chart above, what is the cost
of purchasing exactly cupcakes?

   (A) 5.88
   (B) 6.68
   (C) 8.14
   (D) 8.1
   (E) 9
   (F) 9.53

15. In the figure above, what is the value of
$p + s$?

   (A) 4
   (B) 6
   (C) 8
   (D) 10
   (E) 12

16. In the triangle above, what is the value
of y?

   (A) $\sqrt{4}$
   (B) $5\sqrt{5}$
   (C) $15\sqrt{6}$
   (D) $6\sqrt{3}$
   (E) $4\sqrt{3}$

17. If Y varies directly as ……………,
what is the value of *y* when *m* = 4?

  (A) 0.22
  (B) 0.23
  (C) 0.24
  (D) 0.25
  (E) 0.26

18. If line *k* is the reflection of ………..,
what is the slope of line *k*?

  (A) $-2/3$
  (B) $2/3$
  (C) 0
  (D) 1
  (E) 2

19. In the figure above, what is the value of
x?

  (A) 11
  (B) 12
  (C) 13
  (D) 24
  (E) 36

20. What is the perimeter of the figure
above?

  (A) 34
  (B) 35
  (C) 36
  (D) 41
  (E) 52

Check the Answer Key on the next page.

ANSWER KEY
Mixed Speed Practice Drill: Shortcut #7, #8 and 9

Shortcut Used	Best Choices	Answer	Shortcut Used	Best Choices	Answer
1. Shortcut #8	A, B, or C	A	11. Shortcut #8	A, B or C	B
2. Shortcut #9	B or C	B	12. Shortcut #9	A or B	A
3. Shortcut #9	D or E	E	13. Shortcut #9	A or C	C
4. Shortcut #7	B, C, or D	C	14. Shortcut #9	C or D	D
5. Shortcut #7	B, C, or D	B	15. Shortcut #9	D or E	E
6. Shortcut #7	B, C, or D	C	16. Shortcut #9	D or E	E
7. Shortcut #8	A, B, or C	B	17. Shortcut #7	B, C or D	C
8. Shortcut #7	B, C, or D	D	18. Shortcut #9	A or B	B
9. Shortcut #9	C or D	C	19. Shortcut #8	A, B or C	C
10. Shortcut #8	A, B, or C	A	20. Shortcut #8	A, B or C	A

SCORE BOX

Correct Answers	Raw Points	Scaled Points	Correct Answers	Raw Points	Scaled Points
1	1	10	11	11	110
2	2	20	12	12	120
3	3	30	13	13	130
4	4	40	14	14	140
5	5	50	15	15	150
6	6	60	16	16	160
7	7	70	17	17	170
8	8	80	18	18	180
9	9	90	19	19	190
10	10	100	20	20	200
			____ Your Total	____ Your Raw Points	____ Points Added to Your SAT Score!

SHORTCUT #10: FIND MISTAKES FAST

RULE

The SAT uses each letter choice (A,B,C,D,E) in a section of reading or math questions at least once and at most 8 times.

WHEN a letter choice (A, B, C, D, E) appears in your answers to a reading or math section 8 or more times,

THEN you know exactly which questions to check to find your mistakes.

SECRET PATTERN:

The SAME LETTER CHOICE (A, B, C, D, E) used 8 OR MORE TIMES:

A quick tally of your answer choices to a reading section looks like this:

(A) = 5

(B) = 3

(C) = 10

(D) = 0

(E) = 6

REWARD

The instant you **RECOGNIZE** you selected letter choice **(C)** as your answer to **10** questions, you know exactly **WHERE** to find your mistakes.

Before you start to check your answers in chronological order (*question 1, question 2, question 3*), take a few seconds to tally up the number of times you used each letter choice in a reading or math section (*that contains 20 or more questions*) to instantly identify this **secret pattern: *a letter choice (A, B, C, D, E) used 8 or more times.***

DETECT

the same letter choice used 8 or more times in a Reading or Math Section.

In the tally on the previous page, letter choice (C) was used 10 times.

PREDICT

the questions you answered with the same letter choice 8 or more times contain mistakes (wrong answers).

In the tally on the previous page, the 10 questions you answered with the letter choice (C) contain mistakes.

CHECK

By checking the 8 or more questions you answered with the SAME letter choice (such as: C), you have a near **100% chance** to find a mistake.

If you always mark your answer choices (such as: C and D), you also have a great chance to correct a mistake by changing your answer to your second choice (such as: D). *On the previous page, you could consider changing your answer to 10 questions from your first choice (C) to your second choice.*

SCORE

| 1 correct mistakes | *gives you* | 1(raw) point |
| 1 (raw) point | *roughly adds* | 10 points to your score! |

The following 3 examples give you a snapshot of Shortcut #10. You will see how extremely easy it is to recognize the **error pattern** this Shortcut is based on: **a letter choice is used 8 or more times**.

Example #1: Reading Section

Student Answer Sheet

1. Ⓐ Ⓑ Ⓒ Ⓓ Ⓔ
2. Ⓐ Ⓑ Ⓒ Ⓓ Ⓔ
3. Ⓐ Ⓑ Ⓒ Ⓓ Ⓔ
4. Ⓐ Ⓑ Ⓒ Ⓓ Ⓔ
5. Ⓐ Ⓑ Ⓒ Ⓓ Ⓔ
6. Ⓐ Ⓑ Ⓒ Ⓓ Ⓔ
7. Ⓐ Ⓑ Ⓒ Ⓓ Ⓔ
8. Ⓐ Ⓑ Ⓒ Ⓓ Ⓔ
9. Ⓐ Ⓑ Ⓒ Ⓓ Ⓔ
10. Ⓐ Ⓑ Ⓒ Ⓓ Ⓔ
11. Ⓐ Ⓑ Ⓒ Ⓓ Ⓔ
12. Ⓐ Ⓑ Ⓒ Ⓓ Ⓔ
13. Ⓐ Ⓑ Ⓒ Ⓓ Ⓔ
14. Ⓐ Ⓑ Ⓒ Ⓓ Ⓔ
15. Ⓐ Ⓑ Ⓒ Ⓓ Ⓔ
16. Ⓐ Ⓑ Ⓒ Ⓓ Ⓔ
17. Ⓐ Ⓑ Ⓒ Ⓓ Ⓔ
18. Ⓐ Ⓑ Ⓒ Ⓓ Ⓔ
19. Ⓐ Ⓑ Ⓒ Ⓓ Ⓔ
20. Ⓐ Ⓑ Ⓒ Ⓓ Ⓔ
21. Ⓐ Ⓑ Ⓒ Ⓓ Ⓔ
22. Ⓐ Ⓑ Ⓒ Ⓓ Ⓔ
23. Ⓐ Ⓑ Ⓒ Ⓓ Ⓔ
24. Ⓐ Ⓑ Ⓒ Ⓓ Ⓔ

Student Answer Tally

A = 5
B = 9
C = 1
D = 5
E = 4

Student Mistakes
Check letter choice: **(B)**
Check questions:
8, 11, 12, 13, 15, 17, 19, 21, 23

Example #2: Math Section

Student Answer Sheet

1.	Ⓐ	Ⓑ	**Ⓒ**	Ⓓ	Ⓔ
2.	Ⓐ	Ⓑ	Ⓒ	**Ⓓ**	Ⓔ
3.	Ⓐ	Ⓑ	**Ⓒ**	Ⓓ	Ⓔ
4.	**Ⓐ**	Ⓑ	Ⓒ	Ⓓ	Ⓔ
5.	**Ⓐ**	Ⓑ	Ⓒ	Ⓓ	Ⓔ
6.	Ⓐ	Ⓑ	**Ⓒ**	Ⓓ	Ⓔ
7.	Ⓐ	Ⓑ	Ⓒ	**Ⓓ**	Ⓔ
8.	Ⓐ	Ⓑ	Ⓒ	**Ⓓ**	Ⓔ
9.	**Ⓐ**	Ⓑ	Ⓒ	Ⓓ	Ⓔ
10.	Ⓐ	Ⓑ	Ⓒ	Ⓓ	**Ⓔ**
11.	Ⓐ	Ⓑ	Ⓒ	**Ⓓ**	Ⓔ
12.	Ⓐ	Ⓑ	Ⓒ	**Ⓓ**	Ⓔ
13.	Ⓐ	Ⓑ	Ⓒ	Ⓓ	**Ⓔ**
14.	Ⓐ	Ⓑ	**Ⓒ**	Ⓓ	Ⓔ
15.	Ⓐ	Ⓑ	Ⓒ	Ⓓ	**Ⓔ**
16.	Ⓐ	Ⓑ	Ⓒ	**Ⓓ**	Ⓔ
17.	Ⓐ	Ⓑ	**Ⓒ**	Ⓓ	Ⓔ
18.	Ⓐ	Ⓑ	Ⓒ	**Ⓓ**	Ⓔ
19.	**Ⓐ**	Ⓑ	Ⓒ	Ⓓ	Ⓔ
20.	Ⓐ	Ⓑ	Ⓒ	**Ⓓ**	Ⓔ

Student Answer Tally

A = 4

B = 0

C = 5

D = 8

E = 3

Student Mistakes:

Check letter choice: **(D)**

Check questions:

2, 7, 8, 11, 12, 16, 18, 20

Keep in mind: Since the SAT uses every letter choice at least once, (B) must be the correct answer to at least 1 question in this section.

Example #3: Reading Section

Student Answer Sheet

1. Ⓐ Ⓑ Ⓒ Ⓓ Ⓔ
2. Ⓐ Ⓑ Ⓒ Ⓓ Ⓔ
3. Ⓐ Ⓑ Ⓒ Ⓓ Ⓔ
4. Ⓐ Ⓑ Ⓒ Ⓓ Ⓔ
5. Ⓐ Ⓑ Ⓒ Ⓓ Ⓔ
6. Ⓐ Ⓑ Ⓒ Ⓓ Ⓔ
7. Ⓐ Ⓑ Ⓒ Ⓓ Ⓔ
8. Ⓐ Ⓑ Ⓒ Ⓓ Ⓔ
9. Ⓐ Ⓑ Ⓒ Ⓓ Ⓔ
10. Ⓐ Ⓑ Ⓒ Ⓓ Ⓔ
11. Ⓐ Ⓑ Ⓒ Ⓓ Ⓔ
12. Ⓐ Ⓑ Ⓒ Ⓓ Ⓔ
13. Ⓐ Ⓑ Ⓒ Ⓓ Ⓔ
14. Ⓐ Ⓑ Ⓒ Ⓓ Ⓔ
15. Ⓐ Ⓑ Ⓒ Ⓓ Ⓔ
16. Ⓐ Ⓑ Ⓒ Ⓓ Ⓔ
17. Ⓐ Ⓑ Ⓒ Ⓓ Ⓔ
18. Ⓐ Ⓑ Ⓒ Ⓓ Ⓔ
19. Ⓐ Ⓑ Ⓒ Ⓓ Ⓔ
20. Ⓐ Ⓑ Ⓒ Ⓓ Ⓔ
21. Ⓐ Ⓑ Ⓒ Ⓓ Ⓔ
22. Ⓐ Ⓑ Ⓒ Ⓓ Ⓔ
23. Ⓐ Ⓑ Ⓒ Ⓓ Ⓔ
24. Ⓐ Ⓑ Ⓒ Ⓓ Ⓔ

Student Answer Tally

A = 4
B = 5
C = 3
D = 2
E = 10

Student Mistakes:
Check letter choice: **(E)**
Check questions:
1, 3, 8, 11, 13, 16, 18, 19, 22, 24

The POWER of KNOWING How to Analyze Answer Choices

After seeing Shortcut #10, you have the power of knowing exactly which **secret pattern** to look for in your student answer sheet that will give you an instant opportunity to find and correct mistakes.

Shortcut #10: Speed Practice Drills

Now it is time to practice using Shortcut #10 to access opportunities to score on your SAT in *2 seconds – as fast as you click on Google or tap an app on your smartphone.* The questions in the drills are designed to develop your ability to rapidly scan the answer choices and detect this Shortcut to the answer: *2 answer choices that are alike, except for only 1 difference between them.*

The repetition built into the 3 drills will make scanning the answer choices for Shortcut #10 a part of your test-taking routine – a new habit to FIND MISTAKES FAST. The faster you can snap up Shortcut #10 in the following drills, the better prepared you will be to take advantage of this Shortcut on your SAT test.

No Shortcut is Foolproof

Just as there are exceptions to every rule, you could possibly find an exception to **Shortcut #10**.

Shortcut #10: Speed Practice Drill A

Directions:

▶▶ Set your timer or timer app to 1 minute.

▶▶ Tally the number of times you used each letter choice.

▶▶ Identify the letter(s) you used 8 or more times.

▶▶ Check all the questions you answered with this letter choice to find your mistakes.

Reading Section

Student Answer Sheet

1 Ⓐ Ⓑ Ⓒ Ⓓ ⬤
2 ⬤ Ⓑ Ⓒ Ⓓ Ⓔ
3 Ⓐ Ⓑ Ⓒ Ⓓ ⬤
4 ⬤ Ⓑ Ⓒ Ⓓ Ⓔ
5 Ⓐ Ⓑ ⬤ Ⓓ Ⓔ
6 Ⓐ Ⓑ Ⓒ ⬤ Ⓔ
7 ⬤ Ⓑ Ⓒ Ⓓ Ⓔ
8 Ⓐ ⬤ Ⓒ Ⓓ Ⓔ
9 ⬤ Ⓑ Ⓒ Ⓓ Ⓔ
10 Ⓐ Ⓑ Ⓒ Ⓓ ⬤
11 Ⓐ Ⓑ Ⓒ Ⓓ ⬤
12 Ⓐ Ⓑ Ⓒ ⬤ Ⓔ
13 Ⓐ ⬤ Ⓒ Ⓓ Ⓔ
14 ⬤ Ⓑ Ⓒ Ⓓ Ⓔ
15 Ⓐ Ⓑ Ⓒ Ⓓ ⬤
16 Ⓐ Ⓑ Ⓒ Ⓓ ⬤
17 ⬤ Ⓑ Ⓒ Ⓓ Ⓔ
18 Ⓐ ⬤ Ⓒ Ⓓ Ⓔ
19 ⬤ Ⓑ Ⓒ Ⓓ Ⓔ
20 Ⓐ Ⓑ ⬤ Ⓓ Ⓔ
21 ⬤ Ⓑ Ⓒ Ⓓ Ⓔ
22 Ⓐ Ⓑ ⬤ Ⓓ Ⓔ
23 Ⓐ ⬤ Ⓒ Ⓓ Ⓔ
24 ⬤ Ⓑ Ⓒ Ⓓ Ⓔ

Student Answer Tally

A = _____

B = _____

C = _____

D = _____

E = _____

Student Mistakes

Check letter choice: _____

Check questions: _____

_____

Keep in mind: Since the SAT uses every letter choice at least once, then any letter choice you did not use at least once must be the correct answer to at least 1 question.

Student Answer Sheet	**Student Answer Tally**

Student Answer Sheet		Student Answer Tally
1 Ⓐ Ⓑ **C** Ⓓ Ⓔ		A = _____
2 **A** Ⓑ Ⓒ Ⓓ Ⓔ		
3 Ⓐ Ⓑ Ⓒ **D** Ⓔ		B = _____
4 Ⓐ Ⓑ Ⓒ Ⓓ **E**		
5 Ⓐ Ⓑ Ⓒ **D** Ⓔ		C = _____
6 Ⓐ **B** Ⓒ Ⓓ Ⓔ		
7 Ⓐ Ⓑ Ⓒ **D** Ⓔ		D = _____
8 **A** Ⓑ Ⓒ Ⓓ Ⓔ		
9 Ⓐ Ⓑ Ⓒ **D** Ⓔ		E = _____
10 Ⓐ Ⓑ **C** Ⓓ Ⓔ		
11 Ⓐ Ⓑ **C** Ⓓ Ⓔ		
12 Ⓐ Ⓑ **C** Ⓓ Ⓔ		
13 Ⓐ Ⓑ Ⓒ **D** Ⓔ		
14 Ⓐ Ⓑ Ⓒ **D** Ⓔ		
15 **A** Ⓑ Ⓒ Ⓓ Ⓔ		
16 **A** Ⓑ Ⓒ Ⓓ Ⓔ		
17 Ⓐ Ⓑ Ⓒ **D** Ⓔ		
18 Ⓐ Ⓑ Ⓒ **D** Ⓔ		
19 Ⓐ **B** Ⓒ Ⓓ Ⓔ		
20 Ⓐ Ⓑ Ⓒ **D** Ⓔ		

Student Mistakes

Check letter choice: _____

Check questions: _____

_____

Keep in mind: *Since the SAT uses all the letter choices at least once, then any letter choice you did not use at least once must be the correct answer to at least 1 question.*

Check the Answer Key on the next page.

ANSWER KEY
Shortcut #10: Speed Practice Drill A

Reading Tally

A = **10**

B = 4

C = 3

D = 2

E = 5

Check questions answered
with letter choice **(A)**
to find mistakes

Math Tally

A = 4

B = 4

C = 3

D = 8

E = 1

Check questions answered
with letter choice **(D)**
to find mistakes

Shortcut #10: Speed Practice Drill B

Directions:

▶▶ Set your timer or timer app to 1 minute.

▶▶ Tally the number of times each letter choice is used.

▶▶ Identify the letter choice you used 8 or more times.

▶▶ Check all the question you answered with this letter choice to find your mistakes.

Reading Section

Student Answer Sheet

1. Ⓐ **Ⓑ** Ⓒ Ⓓ Ⓔ
2. Ⓐ Ⓑ Ⓒ **Ⓓ** Ⓔ
3. Ⓐ **Ⓑ** Ⓒ Ⓓ Ⓔ
4. Ⓐ Ⓑ Ⓒ Ⓓ **Ⓔ**
5. **Ⓐ** Ⓑ Ⓒ Ⓓ Ⓔ
6. **Ⓐ** Ⓑ Ⓒ Ⓓ Ⓔ
7. Ⓐ Ⓑ Ⓒ **Ⓓ** Ⓔ
8. Ⓐ Ⓑ Ⓒ Ⓓ **Ⓔ**
9. Ⓐ Ⓑ Ⓒ Ⓓ **Ⓔ**
10. Ⓐ **Ⓑ** Ⓒ Ⓓ Ⓔ
11. Ⓐ Ⓑ Ⓒ **Ⓓ** Ⓔ
12. Ⓐ **Ⓑ** Ⓒ Ⓓ Ⓔ
13. Ⓐ **Ⓑ** Ⓒ Ⓓ Ⓔ
14. Ⓐ Ⓑ **Ⓒ** Ⓓ Ⓔ
15. Ⓐ Ⓑ Ⓒ **Ⓓ** Ⓔ
16. **Ⓐ** Ⓑ Ⓒ Ⓓ Ⓔ
17. Ⓐ Ⓑ Ⓒ Ⓓ **Ⓔ**
18. **Ⓐ** Ⓑ Ⓒ Ⓓ Ⓔ
19. Ⓐ **Ⓑ** Ⓒ Ⓓ Ⓔ
20. Ⓐ **Ⓑ** Ⓒ Ⓓ Ⓔ
21. Ⓐ Ⓑ Ⓒ Ⓓ **Ⓔ**
22. Ⓐ Ⓑ **Ⓒ** Ⓓ Ⓔ
23. Ⓐ **Ⓑ** Ⓒ Ⓓ Ⓔ
24. Ⓐ **Ⓑ** Ⓒ Ⓓ Ⓔ

Student Answer Tally

A = _____

B = _____

C = _____

D = _____

E = _____

Student Mistakes

Check letter choice: _____

Check questions: _____

_____

Keep in mind: *Since the SAT uses all the letter choices at least once, then any letter choice you did not use at least once must be the correct answer to at least 1 question.*

Student Answer Sheet

1. Ⓐ **Ⓑ** Ⓒ Ⓓ Ⓔ
2. Ⓐ Ⓑ Ⓒ **Ⓓ** Ⓔ
3. Ⓐ Ⓑ **Ⓒ** Ⓓ Ⓔ
4. Ⓐ **Ⓑ** Ⓒ Ⓓ Ⓔ
5. Ⓐ Ⓑ **Ⓒ** Ⓓ Ⓔ
6. Ⓐ **Ⓑ** Ⓒ Ⓓ Ⓔ
7. Ⓐ Ⓑ Ⓒ **Ⓓ** Ⓔ
8. Ⓐ Ⓑ **Ⓒ** Ⓓ Ⓔ
9. Ⓐ **Ⓑ** Ⓒ Ⓓ Ⓔ
10. **Ⓐ** Ⓑ Ⓒ Ⓓ Ⓔ
11. Ⓐ **Ⓑ** Ⓒ Ⓓ Ⓔ
12. Ⓐ Ⓑ Ⓒ **Ⓓ** Ⓔ
13. Ⓐ Ⓑ **Ⓒ** Ⓓ Ⓔ
14. Ⓐ Ⓑ Ⓒ Ⓓ **Ⓔ**
15. Ⓐ Ⓑ Ⓒ Ⓓ **Ⓔ**
16. Ⓐ Ⓑ **Ⓒ** Ⓓ Ⓔ
17. Ⓐ Ⓑ Ⓒ Ⓓ **Ⓔ**
18. Ⓐ Ⓑ **Ⓒ** Ⓓ Ⓔ
19. Ⓐ Ⓑ **Ⓒ** Ⓓ Ⓔ
20. Ⓐ Ⓑ **Ⓒ** Ⓓ Ⓔ

Student Answer Tally

A = _____

B = _____

C = _____

D = _____

E = _____

Student Mistakes

Letter Choice to check: _____

Questions to check: _____

_____

Keep in mind: *Since the SAT uses all the letter choices at least once, then any letter choice you did not use at least once must be the correct answer to at least 1 question.*

Check the Answer Key on the next page.

ANSWER KEY
Shortcut #10: Speed Practice Drill B

Reading	Math
A = 4	A = 1
B = 9	B = 5
C = 2	**C = 8**
D = 4	D = 3
E = 5	E = 3

Check questions answered
with letter choice **(B)**
to find mistakes

Check questions answered
with letter choice **(C)**
to find mistakes

Shortcut #10: Speed Practice Drill C

Directions:

▶▶ Set your timer or timer app to 1 minute.

▶▶ Tally the number of times each letter choice is used.

▶▶ Identify the letter choice you used 8 or more times.

▶▶ Check all the questions you answered with this letter choice to find your mistakes.

Reading Section

Student Answer Sheet

1 Ⓐ Ⓑ Ⓒ Ⓓ Ⓔ
2 Ⓐ Ⓑ Ⓒ Ⓓ Ⓔ
3 Ⓐ Ⓑ Ⓒ Ⓓ Ⓔ
4 Ⓐ Ⓑ Ⓒ Ⓓ Ⓔ
5 Ⓐ Ⓑ Ⓒ Ⓓ Ⓔ
6 Ⓐ Ⓑ Ⓒ Ⓓ Ⓔ
7 Ⓐ Ⓑ Ⓒ Ⓓ Ⓔ
8 Ⓐ Ⓑ Ⓒ Ⓓ Ⓔ
9 Ⓐ Ⓑ Ⓒ Ⓓ Ⓔ
10 Ⓐ Ⓑ Ⓒ Ⓓ Ⓔ
11 Ⓐ Ⓑ Ⓒ Ⓓ Ⓔ
12 Ⓐ Ⓑ Ⓒ Ⓓ Ⓔ
13 Ⓐ Ⓑ Ⓒ Ⓓ Ⓔ
14 Ⓐ Ⓑ Ⓒ Ⓓ Ⓔ
15 Ⓐ Ⓑ Ⓒ Ⓓ Ⓔ
16 Ⓐ Ⓑ Ⓒ Ⓓ Ⓔ
17 Ⓐ Ⓑ Ⓒ Ⓓ Ⓔ
18 Ⓐ Ⓑ Ⓒ Ⓓ Ⓔ
19 Ⓐ Ⓑ Ⓒ Ⓓ Ⓔ
20 Ⓐ Ⓑ Ⓒ Ⓓ Ⓔ
21 Ⓐ Ⓑ Ⓒ Ⓓ Ⓔ
22 Ⓐ Ⓑ Ⓒ Ⓓ Ⓔ
23 Ⓐ Ⓑ Ⓒ Ⓓ Ⓔ
24 Ⓐ Ⓑ Ⓒ Ⓓ Ⓔ

Student Answer Tally

A = _____

B = _____

C = _____

D = _____

E = _____

Student Mistakes

Check letter choice: _____

Check questions: _____

_____

Keep in mind: *Since the SAT uses all the letter choices at least once, then any letter choice you did not use at least once, must be the correct answer to at least 1 question.*

Math Section

Student Answer Sheet

1 Ⓐ Ⓑ Ⓒ ① Ⓔ
2 Ⓐ Ⓑ Ⓒ Ⓓ Ⓔ
3 Ⓐ Ⓑ Ⓒ Ⓓ Ⓔ
4 Ⓐ Ⓑ Ⓒ Ⓓ Ⓔ
5 Ⓐ Ⓑ Ⓒ Ⓓ Ⓔ
6 Ⓐ Ⓑ Ⓒ Ⓓ Ⓔ
7 Ⓐ Ⓑ Ⓒ Ⓓ Ⓔ
8 Ⓐ Ⓑ Ⓒ Ⓓ Ⓔ
9 Ⓐ Ⓑ Ⓒ Ⓓ Ⓔ
10 Ⓐ Ⓑ Ⓒ Ⓓ Ⓔ
11 Ⓐ Ⓑ Ⓒ Ⓓ Ⓔ
12 Ⓐ Ⓑ Ⓒ Ⓓ Ⓔ
13 Ⓐ Ⓑ Ⓒ Ⓓ Ⓔ
14 Ⓐ Ⓑ Ⓒ Ⓓ Ⓔ
15 Ⓐ Ⓑ Ⓒ Ⓓ Ⓔ
16 Ⓐ Ⓑ Ⓒ Ⓓ Ⓔ
17 Ⓐ Ⓑ Ⓒ Ⓓ Ⓔ
18 Ⓐ Ⓑ Ⓒ Ⓓ Ⓔ
19 Ⓐ Ⓑ Ⓒ Ⓓ Ⓔ
20 Ⓐ Ⓑ Ⓒ Ⓓ Ⓔ

Student Answer Tally

A = _____

B = _____

C = _____

D = _____

E = _____

Student Mistakes

Check letter choice: _____

Check questions: _____

_____

Keep in mind: *Since the SAT uses all the letter choices at least once, then a letter choice you did not use at least once must be the correct answer to at least 1 question.*

Check the Answer Key on the next page.

ANSWER KEY
Shortcut #10: Speed Practice Drill C

Reading	Math
A = 5	A = 2
B = 3	B = 5
C = 4	**C = 8**
D = 8	D = 3
E = 4	E = 2

Check questions answered
with letter choice (**D**)
to find mistakes

Check questions answered
with letter choice (**C**)
to find mistakes

Practice in Your SAT Workbooks

After completing the 3 practice drills, you are the ***all-seeing, all-knowing,*** newly-minted **MASTER** of Shortcut #10. Now you can put it to work for you.

Go to any SAT workbook and scan the answer keys to reading or math sections that have 20 or more questions and you will see: 1) every letter choice is used at least once and 2) no letter choice is used more than 8 times in a section. The more you see this pattern in the answer keys, the more confident you will be checking the letter choice you selected 8 or more times for mistakes (*wrong answers*).

Nike tells you: ***Just do it!***

Dr. Jay tells you: ***Just use it!***

Just use it on every practice test you take, and you will be ready to snap up Shortcut #10 hidden inside your SAT test.

Even if you don't use 1 letter choice 8 or more times, look to the letter choice you used the most throughout the questions for errors. Maybe you used it 7 times and not 8. This is still the first place to look for mistakes.

PART III
TOP 4 SAT VOCABULARY
SECRETS

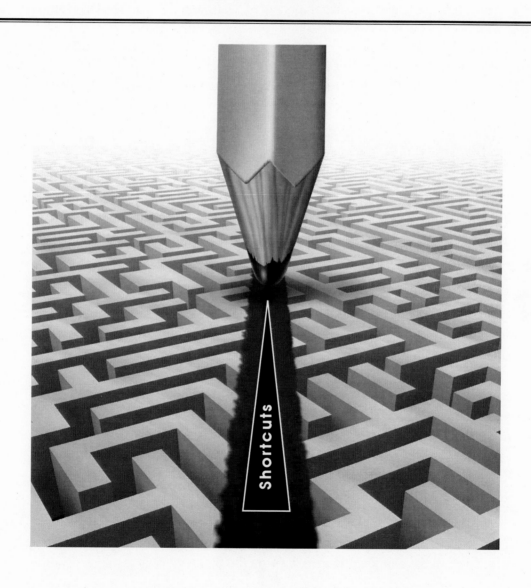

Shortcuts

SHORTCUTS

Top 4
SAT Vocabulary Secrets

Vocabulary development is a gargantuan component of SAT prep. There are just as many SAT vocabulary workbooks as there are SAT test-prep workbooks. But, there is only so much time you can devote to developing your SAT vocabulary. Here are 4 vocabulary secrets that will immediately save you time and simplify your approach to learning SAT vocabulary. ***The more vocabulary secrets you know, the less you will stress over the words you will see on your SAT.***

 SAT Vocabulary Secret #1: All the SAT Words You Really Need to Know are in the Answer Choices

STOP thinking you should know the meaning of every odd word you come across in print, online, or hear anywhere.

START focusing on learning the meaning of all the words in the answer choices to SAT questions.

If you have taken a couple of practice tests, you have already seen some of the more challenging words that often appear in the answer choices, such as: ***ambiguous, capricious, cynical, equitable,*** and ***garrulous***. Be sure you know the meaning of these words and all the words in the answer choices.

Put this vocabulary secret to work on all your practice tests. Make it your TOP PRIORITY to learn the meaning of ALL the words in the answer choices you cannot define. ***The more words in the answer choices you can define, the easier it is to answer SAT questions.***

 SAT Vocabulary Secret #2: All You Really Need to Know about SAT Words is a Basic, 1-Word Definition or Synonym.

STOP thinking you need to develop ***in-depth knowledge*** of the meaning of words to be prepared to answer all the challenging questions on the SAT.

START thinking you only need to develop a ***basic knowledge*** of the meaning of words to be prepared to answer all the challenging questions on the SAT.

The basic knowledge you need to answer SAT questions is a 1-word definition or synonym. For example, you need to know that the word "capricious" means "changeable," but it is not necessary to know that "capricious" also means fickle, volatile, and mercurial.

The 1-word definition "changeable" gives you *just enough information* about what "capricious" means for you to be able to either: 1) eliminate this word in the answer choices to a question, or 2) consider this word a possible answer to a question.

Put this vocabulary secret to work on all your practice tests. Notice how little information about a word you actually use when you answer a question.

 ## SAT Vocabulary Secret #3: Little Negative Prefixes Are a Big Clue to Answer SAT Questions.

STOP thinking: I cannot answer an SAT question if I do not know the meaning of all the words in the answer choices

START thinking: I can answer SAT questions when I do not know the meaning of all the words in the answer choices by using negative prefixes to partially define words as having a negative meaning.

The negative prefixes *dis, im, in, ir,* and *un* are frequently added to the beginning of words in the answer choices to SAT questions. When a negative prefix such as *dis* is added to a word like *dis*agree, it changes the meaning of the root word to "not" or "the opposite of," as in: *dis*agree means **not** agree or **the opposite of** agreeing.

When you see the negative prefix "*dis*" at the beginning of words such as *dis*concerting, *dis*dain and *dis*parity or the negative prefix *in* at the beginning of words such as *in*conspicuous, *in*credulous or *in*discriminate, the prefixes tell you these words have a negative meaning. This is *just enough information* to partially define these words and answer questions on your SAT you previously skipped.

The following example illustrates how the frequently used negative prefixes *dis* and *in* give you *just enough information* to either eliminate a negative word in the answer choices or consider a negative word as a possible answer to a question.

Example: Negative Prefix Clue

Compared to the tone in Passage 1, the tone of Passage 2 is more:

(A) scholarly

(B) *in*tolerant

(C) respectful

(D) *dis*dainful

(E) sympathetic

All you really need to know about the meaning of *in*tolerant and *dis*dainful to eliminate (B) and (D) in the answer choices or identify (B) and (D) as the 2 most likely answers to a question is that these 2 words have a negative meaning. If the feeling you take away from Passage 2 is more negative than Passage 1, then (B) or (D) is the answer to the question. You have a 50/50 change to correctly answer the question by selecting (B) or (D) *–without knowing the actual meaning of the word "intolerant" or "disdainful!"*

Put this vocabulary secret to work on all your practice tests. Start by scanning the answer choices to questions in any reading section of a practice test and seeing several examples of words that begin with the negative prefixes *dis, im, in, ir,* and *un.* **The more negative prefixes you use to partially define SAT words as "negative," the more SAT questions you can answer —** *without knowing the actual meaning of all the words in the answer choices.*

 ## SAT Vocabulary Secret #4: You Can Instantly Memorize the Meaning of SAT Words by Using Triple-Letter-Links

STOP slowly memorizing words by reading and writing the words over and over again.

START instantly memorizing words by using Dr. Jay's mnemonic device called Triple-Letter-Links.

Triple-Letter-Links speeds up the process of memorizing the basic meaning of SAT words by matching the first 3 letters at the beginning of a *unfamiliar* **SAT word** with the first three letters at the beginning of a *familiar* **word** in your vocabulary.

The use of the same 3 letters at the beginning of both the unfamiliar and familiar word creates a strong visual clue that sticks in your mind like glue and makes it possible for you to memorize the meaning of a SAT word in a matter of seconds.

Triple-Letter-Links 100

Challenge yourself to use Triple-Letter-Links to memorize the basic meaning of words in the following list. Give top priority to memorizing the meaning of words you have seen in the answer choices to SAT questions. Many words in this list may look familiar to you from practice tests, but you may not be able to actually define them. Now is the time to quickly learn the basic meaning. Memorize a word in 30 seconds. Add 2 words to your vocabulary in 1 minute, 60 words in 30 minutes!

SAT Word	Triple Letter Links	Basic Meaning
1. accrue (v.)	*link* acc *with* accumulate	accumulate
2. alleviate (v.)	link allev with Aleve or	relieve
3. antiquated (adj.)	link antiq with antique	old
4. applicable (adj.)	link app with applied	able to be applied
5. arduous (adj.)	link ard with hard	difficult
6. artisan (n.)	link arti with artist	artist
7. assimilation (n.)	link simil with similar	make similar
8. audible (adj.)	link aud with audio	able to be heard
9. banish (v.)	link ban with banned books	throw out

| 10. | benevolent (adj.) | link **bene** with **beneficial** | **benefitting others** |

| 11. | **bla**nd (adj.) | link **bla** with **tastes bla** | **mild** |

| 12. | **boo**rish (adj.) | link **boo** with **booing** | **rude** |

| 13. | **brea**ch (n.) | link **brea** with **break** | **break a law** |

| 14. | **bre**vity (adj.) | link **bre** with **brief** | **brief** |

| 15. | **bro**ach (v.) | link **br** with **bring up** | **bring up a subject** |

| 16. | **cap**ricious (adj.) | link **cap** with **changing caps** | **changeable** |

| 17. | **car**icature (n.) | link **car** with **cartoon** | **(cartoon) sketch** |

| 18. | **chi**de (v.) | link **chi** with scold a **child** | **scold** |

| 19. | **circu**itous (adj.) | link **circu** with **circular** | **round about** |

| 20. | **copi**ous (adj.) | link **copi** with many **copies** | **plentiful** |

| 21. | **cover**t (adj.) | link **cover** with **cover up** | **concealed** |

| 22. | **cred**ible (adj.) | link **cred** with **creed & beliefs** | **believable** |

23. dormant (adj.)	link dorm with sleep	inactive
24. dubious (adj.)	link dub with doubt	doubtful
25. duplicity (n.)	link dup with duped	deceive
26. durable (adj.)	link dur with enduring	lasting
27. dutiful (adj.)	link duti with duty	obedient
28. edify (v.)	link ed with educate	educate
29. efficacious (adj.)	link eff with effective	effective
30. egocentric (adj.)	link ego with self	self-centered
31. enervate (v.)	link ener with drain energy	drain strength
32. erroneous (adj.)	link erro with error	wrong
33. equitable (adj.)	link equ with equal	fair
34. escalation (n.)	link escal with escalator	rising intensity
35. exemplary (adj.)	link exempl with example	good example

36.	extraneous (adj.)	link **extra** with **excessive**	excessive
37.	façade (n.)	link **fac** with **face**	**outward appearance**
38.	fallacy (n.)	link **fal** with **false**	**falsehood, untruth**
39.	flaccid (adj.)	link **fla** with **flabby**	**flabby**
40.	fortuitous (adj.)	link **fortu** with **fortune**	**by chance**
41.	frenetic (adj.)	link **fren** with **frenzied**	**frenzied**
42.	garrulous (adj.)	link **gar** with **Gary is talkative**	talkative
43.	genteel (adj.)	link **gent** with **gentleman**	**polished**
44.	glacial (adj.)	link **glac** with **glacier**	ice
45.	grievious (adj.)	link **grie** with **grief**	**causing grief**
46.	imminent (adj.)	link **imm** with **immediate**	**about to happen**
47.	impetuous (adj.)	link **imp** with **impulsive**	**impulsive**
48.	judicious (adj.)	link **jud** with **judge**	**sound judgment**

49.	laborious (adj.)	link **labor** with **work**	hard work

50.	lackluster (adj.)	link **lack** with **lack brightness**	dull

51.	longevity (n.)	link **long** with **long life**	long life

52.	magnanimous (adj.)	link **magni** with **magnificently kind**	magnificently kind, generous

53.	mediocre (adj.)	link **medi** with **medium**	medium quality

54.	mystic (adj.)	link **myst** with **mysterious**	mysterious

55.	negligible (adj.)	link **negl** with **can neglect**	little value

56.	ominous (adj.)	link **omin** with **bad omen**	foreshadowing evil

57.	pallid (adj.)	link **pal** with **pale**	pale

58.	perilous (adj.)	link **peril** with **dangerous**	dangerous

59.	pertinent (adj.)	link **pert** with **pertains to**	relevant

60.	plethora (n.)	link **ple** with **plentiful**	excessive

61.	pragmatic (adj.)	link **pra** with **practical**	practical

| 62. | pretentious (adj.) | link **preten** with **pretend** | **pretend to be important** |

| 63. | propriety (n.) | link **propr** with **proper** | **proper behavior** |

| 64. | punitive (adj.) | link **puni** with **punish** | **inflict punishment** |

| 65. | purge (v.) | link **pur** with **purify** | **cleanse** |

| 66. | query (n.) | link **que** with **question** | **question** |

| 67. | quiescent (adj.) | link **quie** with **quiet** | **quiet** |

| 68. | replenish (v.) | link **repl** with **replace** | **replace** |

| 69. | respite (n.) | link **res** with **rest** | **temporary rest** |

| 70. | revere (v.) | link **rever** with **reverence** | **regard with reverence** |

| 71. | sacrosanct (adj.) | link **sacr** with **sacred** | **hold sacred** |

| 72. | sagacious (adj.) | link **sag** with **sage** | **wise** |

| 73. | satiate (adj.) | link **sati** with **satisfied** | **completely full** |

| 74. | serpentine (adj.) | link **serpent** with **snake** | **snakelike** |

75. **serv**ile (adj.)	link **serv** with **servant** who is	**submissive**
76. **slo**venly (adj.)	link **slo** with **sloppy**	**sloppy**
77. **solid**arity (n.)	link **solid** with **solid** support	**unity**
78. **son**orous (adj.)	link **son** with **sound**	**producing sound**
79. **spa**tial (adj.)	link **spa** with **space**	**occur in space**
80. **strat**agem (n.)	link **strat** with **strategy**	**strategy to deceive**
81. **stri**ngent (adj.)	link **stri** with **strict**	**strict**
82. **stu**por (n.)	link **stu** with **stun**	**stunned condition**
83. **suffi**ce (v.)	link **suffi** with **sufficient**	**sufficient**
84. **sul**len (adj.)	link **sul** with **sulk**	**sulky**
85. **super**cilious (adj.)	link **super** with **superior**	**act superior**
86. **terr**estrial (adj.)	link **terr** with **terrain**	**related to Earth**
87. **tim**orous (adj.)	link **tim** with **timid**	**timid**

88.	totalitarian (adj.)	link **total** with **total control**	**total control**
89.	trepidation (n.)	link **tre** with **tremble**	**trembling**
90.	valorous (adj.)	link **val** with **valiant**	**valiant**
91.	vacuous (adj.)	link **vacu** with **vacuum**	**empty**
92.	variegated (adj.)	link **varie** with **varied**	**varied in appearance**
93.	verbose (adj.)	link **verb** with **words**	**wordy**
94.	vigilant (adj.)	link **vigil** with **keep a vigil**	**watchful**
95.	vilify (v.)	link **vil** with **villain**	**make evil statements**
96.	virulent (adj.)	link **vir** with **virus**	**highly infectious**
97.	vociferous (adj.)	link **voc** with **vocal**	**shouting voice**
98.	volatile (adj.)	link **vol** with **volcano**	**explosive**
99.	voluminous (adj)	link **volum** with **volume**	**great volume**
100.	wistful (adj.)	link **wis** with **wishful**	**wishful, longing for**

Now that you have experienced how rapidly you can memorize the basic meaning of 100 SAT words by using *Dr. Jay's Triple-Letter-Links Memorization Strategy*, come back tomorrow to experience how many words you will recall.

Make Your Own Triple-Letter-Links

Come up with your own **Triple-Letter-Links** to turn hard SAT words you encounter into easy words you can memorize in seconds. The **Triple-Letter-Links** do not have to be at the beginning of a word. You can link any letters in a SAT word to a basic one-word definition or synonym. The first 3 letters at the beginning of a word are a particularly strong visual memory clue and an easy place to start to create Triple-Letter-Links. You can also use letters in the middle or end of SAT words as visual memory clues, as the following examples illustrate:

SAT Word	Letter Links	Basic Meaning
1. relin**qui**sh (v.)	link **qui** with **quit**	give up
2. de**ride** (v.)	link **rid** with **ridicule**	ridicule
3. en**light**ened (v.)	link **light** with **see the light**	insightful
4. de**cry** (v.)	link **cry** with **cry out against**	condemn
5. for**bear**ance (n.)	link **bear** with **bear with**	patience

PART IV
YOUR POWER-SCORING GEAR

Shortcuts

SHORTCUTS

The Master Game Plan

Now you are at the top of your game. In addition to POE and all of the SAT skills you have developed from all of your teachers and tutors, workbooks and courses, you now have the *extra scoring power* of **10 Shortcuts** and **4 vocabulary secrets** to add 100 points or more to your SAT score. You have SHORTCUTS plus POE = the winning combination of strategies to maximize your success.

You have developed the habit of taking 2 seconds to scan SAT questions for a Shortcut. Scanning the answer choices for Dr. Jay's top 10 Shortcuts is your new, first step to find more answers and super-size your SAT score.

Top10 Shortcuts

READING SHORTCUT #1: is a silver lining inside an SAT question that gives you a golden opportunity to score a point when you SEE **the same word(s) at the beginning of 2 answer choices**.

When 2 answer choices in a reading question begin with the same word(s), you can now predict that the answer is most likely 1 of these 2 choices.

READING SHORTCUT #2: is a silver lining inside an SAT question that gives you a golden opportunity to score a point when you SEE **the same word(s) at the end of 2 answer choices**.

When 2 answer choices in a reading question end with the same word(s), you can now predict that the answer is most likely 1 of these 2 choices.

READING SHORTCUT #3: is a silver lining inside an SAT question that gives you a golden opportunity to score a point when you SEE **2 answer choices that have the same word(s) in different locations**.

When 2 answer choices in a reading question contain the same word(s) in different locations, you can now predict that the answer is most likely 1 of these 2 choices.

READING SHORTCUT #4: is a **silver lining** inside an SAT question that gives you a golden opportunity to score a point when you SEE **a word(s) in the italicized Introduction matches a word(s) in 1 answer choice.**

When a word(s) in the italicized Introduction to a passage matches a word(s) in 1 answer choice, then you can now predict the exact answer.

READING SHORTCUT #5: is a **silver lining** inside an SAT question that gives you a golden opportunity to score a point when you SEE **the answer choices that match the tone of the passage**.

When 2 or 3 words in the answer choices match the tone or feeling you take away from a passage, then you can now predict that 1 of those answer choices is correct.

WRITING SHORTCUT #6: is a **silver lining** inside an SAT question that gives you a golden opportunity to score a point when you SEE **answer choice (A) ends with the same word(s) as 1 other answer choice**.

When answer choice (A) and another answer choice end with the same words and are almost a perfect match, you can now predict that 1 of the 2 choices is most likely the correct answer.

MATH SHORTCUT #7: is a **silver lining** inside an SAT question that gives you a golden opportunity to score a point when you SEE **ALL 5 answer choices are consecutive numbers.**

When a math question answer choices all are in consecutive order, (such as (A)12 (B)13 (C)14 (D)15 (E)16), you can now predict that (B), (C), or (D) is the correct answer.

MATH SHORTCUT #8: is a **silver lining** inside an SAT question that gives you a golden opportunity to score a point when you SEE **ONLY the first 3 answer choices are consecutive numbers**.

When only the first 3 answer choices are in consecutive order, (such as (A) 1, (B) 2, and (C) 3), you can now predict that (A), (B), or (C) is the correct answer.

MATH SHORTCUT #9: is a **silver lining** inside an SAT question that gives you a golden opportunity to score a point when you SEE **2 answer choices that are alike, except for only 1 difference**.

When a math question has 2 answer choices that are the same except for 1 difference between them (such as 25 and 25.5), you can now predict that 1 of these 2 answer choices is the most likely the correct answer.

SHORTCUT #10: is a **silver lining** inside an SAT question that gives you a golden opportunity to correct mistakes when you SEE **the same letter choice in your answers to 8 or more questions in a section.**

When the same letter choice appears in your answer to 8 or more questions within a section, you now know exactly where to find your mistakes.

TOP 4 Vocabulary Secrets

Dr. Jay's top 4 vocabulary secrets are now part of your strategy to simplify answering SAT questions:

SAT Vocabulary Secret #1: Focus on Answer Choice Words

The most important SAT words you need to know are the words that appear in the answer choices. The instant you focus on the words in the answer choices and see how few words you need to learn, the less stressed you will be about your SAT vocabulary.

SAT Vocabulary Secret #2: Learn Just Basic Definitions

All you really need to know about the meaning of SAT vocabulary words to answer SAT questions is just a basic definition. When you know just a basic definition of a word, you can either eliminate an answer choice or consider an answer choice as possibly the best answer to a question.

SAT Vocabulary Secret #3: Use Negative Prefixes

Many SAT words in the answer choices begin with a negative *prefix*, (such as *dis, im, in, ir, or un*), The instant you use a negative prefix to partially define a word, the *easier* it is to answer SAT reading questions.

SAT Vocabulary Secret #4: Use Triple-Letter-Links

When you use triple letters to give you a clue to the meaning of a word, then you can memorize the basic meaning of an SAT word in a matter of seconds.

Secret Codes: Review Before the Test

All the **secret patterns** underlying the Shortcuts are now your **Secret Codes**. Take a moment to put a snapshot of the Secret Codes in your cellphone. The codes will instantly remind you of the patterns in the answer choices that give you Shortcuts to the answers.

S#1 Secret Code: (A) **provide** xxxxxxxxx

                                   (B) **provide** xxxxxxxx

S#2 Secret Code: (C) xxxxxx **train**

                                   (E) xxxxxx **train**

S#3 Secret Code: (D) xxxxxxxx**returned** xxxxx

                                   (E) xx **returned** xxxxxxxxxx

----

S#4 Secret Code: Introduction: *On a* **journey** *to America*

                                   (E) **journey**

S#5 Secret Code: Passage: **negative** tone or feeling ....

                                   (A) **skeptical**

                                   (B) **apprehensive**

                                   Passage: **positive** tone or feeling ....

                                   (C) **encouraging**

                                   (E) **open-minded**

S#6 Secret Code: (A) the department store was **crowded with shoppers**

                        (B) the department store is **crowded with shoppers**

S#7 Secret Code: **(A) 1**

                        (B) 2

                        (C) 3

                        (D) 4

                        (E) 5

S#8 Secret Code: **(A) 1**

                        (B) 2

                        (C) 3

S#9 Secret Code: **(B) 12.5**

                        (D) 12

S#10 Secret Code: **(A) = 4**

                        (B) = 3

                        (C) = 3

                        (D) = 9

                        (E) = 5

Whenever you start stressing about the SAT, go to your **Secret Codes** to REFRESH your memory of your favorite Shortcuts that give you the extra scoring power you want to have on your test day.

FAST FORWARD to Your Test Day

As I always say to my students:

May the Shortcuts be with you!

Walk IN to YOUR SAT

with THE GOLDEN RULE to Maximize Your Score:

Always take 2 seconds to look for a Shortcut!

Walk OUT of Your SAT

Knowing you took advantage of at least 10 Shortcuts

to collect at least 50 EXTRA points

to open the doors of more colleges to you.

SHORTCUTS

INDEX

About the Author

Carol Jay Stratoudakis, Ph.D., known as Dr. Jay, has developed a simple, pattern-based strategy that gives test-takers the power to use Shortcuts to find answers fast and easily increase their scores on the SAT, ACT, GRE, GMAT, LSAT, and many other high-stakes, multiple-choice tests.

Dr. Jay's strategy draws upon her pattern-based approach to teaching "at risk" students how to read, her experience teaching SAT test prep, and her dissertation research at Michigan State University through the Institute for Research on Teaching. Dr. Jay's experience in student assessment at the elementary, middle school, high school, and university level all contribute to her expertise in decoding patterns in tests and reducing complex test questions to their simplest form.

Dr. Jay's national experience related to assessment includes working on teacher evaluation research at the National Institute of Education, authoring a series of articles for The National Staff Development Council, and serving as a consultant to the National Education Goals Panel where she contributed to the publication of a national report on common standards in American education, a benchmark report preceding the Common Core Standards. Dr. Jay has also served as a consultant on educational assessment to the Connecticut Department of Education and the Commonwealth of Massachusetts Department of Education.

Dr. Jay is creating more Shortcuts for the 2016 SAT. Check her website: info@ DrJaySATShortcuts.com for Shortcut updates, to share comments on your favorite Shortcuts, and to see where she is doing a Shortcut demonstration. Dr. Jay lives in Fairfax, Virginia, with her husband who is a psychologist.